HSE
Health & Safety
Executive

A guide to the Reporting of Injuries, Diseases and Dangerous Occurrences Regulations 1995

L73

HSE BOOKS

First published 1996

ISBN 0 7176 1012 8

This publication includes guidance issued by the Health and Safety Executive. Following the guidance is not compulsory and you are free to take other action. But if you do follow the guidance you will normally be doing enough to comply with the law. Health and safety inspectors seek to secure compliance with the law and may refer to this guidance as illustrating good practice.

Contents

Introduction

1 This publication gives detailed guidance on The Reporting of Injuries, Diseases and Dangerous Occurrences Regulations 1995 (RIDDOR 1995), which come into force on 1 April 1996.

2 The Regulations are made under the Health and Safety at Work etc Act 1974 (HSW Act). They consolidate and simplify the law by applying a single set of reporting requirements to all work activities in Great Britain and in the offshore oil and gas industry. The main purpose of the Regulations is to generate reports to the Health and Safety Executive (HSE) and to local authorities. The reports provide data which is used to indicate where and how risks arise and to show up trends. This enables the enforcing authorities to target their activities effectively and to advise employers on strategies to help prevent injuries, ill health and accidental loss.

3 This publication is produced together with a free leaflet *Everyone's guide to RIDDOR '95*[1]. The leaflet contains all the information most people will need to appreciate their duties and identify when they must act. This guide contains more detailed technical background information and advice on interpretation. It will be of particular interest to safety professionals.

4 The guide is set out as follows:

- summary of the main requirements;
- summary of the key changes from RIDDOR 1985;
- full text of the Regulations and schedules, together with detailed guidance notes.

5 A separate, detailed guide is available on the application of the Regulations to railways, tramways, trolley vehicle systems and guided transport systems[2].

Summary of the main duties

6 This section summarises what the Regulations require and gives pointers to more detailed notes accompanying the full text of the Regulations.

7 The Regulations apply to events which arise out of or in connection with work activities covered by the HSW Act. The terms 'work' and 'at work' are defined in the HSW Act, as modified by the Health and Safety (Training for Employment) Regulations 1990 and include work as an employee or self-employed person, work experience provided in connection with a training course or programme (except 'simulated' work experience provided directly by an educational establishment on its premises as part of a course) and training for employment. An extended definition of 'at work' applies for the purposes of these Regulations to people at offshore workplaces (see regulation 2(3)).

8 Whenever any of the following events arises 'out of or in connection with work' (see regulation 2(2)(c) and paragraph 33), it must be reported to the enforcing authority in writing and a record kept (see regulation 7 and paragraph 86). If (a), (b), (c) or (d) happens the enforcing authority must first be notified by the quickest practicable means (eg by telephone):

(a) the death of *any person* as a result of an accident, whether or not they are at work (see regulation 3(1) and paragraph 43);

(b) someone who is at work suffers a major injury as a result of an accident (see regulation 3(1) and paragraph 44). Major injuries are listed in Schedule 1;

(c) someone who is not at work (eg a member of the public) suffers an injury as a result of an accident and is taken from the scene to a hospital for treatment, or, if the accident happens at a hospital, suffers a major injury (see regulation 3(1) and paragraphs 45 and 47);

(d) one of a list of specified dangerous occurrences takes place (see regulation 3(1)and paragraph 48). Dangerous occurrences are events which do not necessarily result in a reportable injury, but have the potential to do significant harm. They are listed in Schedule 2;

(e) someone at work is unable to do their normal work for more than 3 days as a result of an injury (an 'over-3-day' injury) caused by an accident at work (see regulation 3(2) and paragraph 55);

(f) the death of an employee if this occurs some time after a reportable injury which led to that employee's death, but not more than one year afterwards (see regulation 4 and paragraph 61); or

(g) a person at work suffers one of a number of specified diseases, provided that a doctor diagnoses the disease and (except for certain communicable diseases reportable only offshore) the person's job involves a specified work activity (see regulation 5 and paragraph 64). The specified diseases and corresponding work activities are set out in Schedule 3. Those reportable only offshore are listed in part 2 of that Schedule.

9 The duty to notify and report these events rests with the 'responsible person'. The 'responsible person' is defined in regulation 2 and may (although special arrangements apply in the case of a mine, quarry, closed tip, diving operation, offshore installation, well, pipe-line or road vehicle carrying a dangerous substance) be the employer of an injured person, a self-employed

person, or someone in control of premises where work is carried on (this will depend on the circumstances and on who dies or suffers a reportable injury or disease). Guidance on this is given in paragraphs 25 to 31.

10 In addition to the requirements outlined in paragraph 8, regulation 6 (see guidance at paragraph 74) requires that a report must be made in the following circumstances:

(a) a conveyor of flammable gas through a fixed pipe distribution system or the filler, importer or supplier of liquefied petroleum gas (LPG) in a refillable container, must report if they learn that someone has died or suffered a major injury arising out of, or in connection with that gas - unless the death or injury falls within the scope of regulation 3(1);

(b) any registered installation business must report if it finds that there is, in any premises, a gas fitting or associated flue or ventilation arrangement which could be dangerous in a way specified in regulation 6(2).

Where the Regulations apply

11 The Regulations apply to Great Britain but not to Northern Ireland where separate but identical Regulations will be made. They also apply to certain work activities carried out in United Kingdom territorial waters adjacent to Great Britain and in the United Kingdom sector of the Continental Shelf (see Regulation 12). These are the work activities specified by the Health and Safety at Work etc Act 1974 (Application outside Great Britain) Order 1995 (the 1995 Order), which include for example: offshore installations; wells; pipelines and pipeline works; and related activities. The Regulations also apply to mines under the sea and certain other activities in territorial waters, such as: the loading and unloading of ships; the construction and repair of ships; the construction and repair of buildings or other structures; and certain diving operations.

Key changes

12 RIDDOR 1995 replaces the Reporting of Injuries, Diseases and Dangerous Occurrences Regulations 1985 (RIDDOR 1985), the Railways (Notice of Accidents) Order 1986, and certain provisions of the Offshore Installations (Inspectors and Casualties) Regulations 1973 and the Submarine Pipelines (Inspectors etc) Regulations 1977. Certain provisions of the Regulation of Railways Act 1871 and the Transport and Works Act 1992 are also repealed or amended.

13 The main areas of change over the reporting requirements in RIDDOR 1985 are:

(a) accident (*regulation 2(1)*) has been defined to include acts of violence done to people at work and acts of suicide on railways or other relevant transport systems;

(b) reportable injuries to people not at work (eg members of the public) are now deaths, and any injuries which cause a person to be taken from the site of the accident to a hospital. However, if the accident occurs out of or in connection with work at a hospital then to be reportable it must be a defined major injury (*regulation 3(1)(a),(c) and (d)*). (Accidents arising directly out of the conduct of medical treatment by a doctor or dentist continue to be excluded (*regulation 10)*);

(c) the list of reportable major injuries has been revised and simplified (*Schedule 1*);

(d) the list of dangerous occurrences which must be reported (*Schedule 2*) has been updated: it consists of general provisions as well as additional occurrences reportable in respect of mines, quarries, relevant transport systems and offshore workplaces;

(e) the list of reportable diseases has been updated. A list of diseases additionally reportable only offshore has also been added to it (*regulation 5 and Schedule 3*);

(f) the report required to be sent to the enforcing authority may be sent either on a form approved by the Executive or by some other means approved by the Executive (*regulation 3(1)(ii) and 5(1)*). This enables the Executive to approve the sending of reports by, for instance, telephone. Any such change to the reporting arrangements would be widely publicised;

(g) people responsible for reporting gas incidents include those approved under the Gas Safety (Installation and Use) Regulations 1994 (*regulation 6(2)*);

(h) the Health and Safety Executive is given limited power to grant exemptions from requirements imposed by the Regulations (*regulation 13*).

Regulation 1

Citation and commencement

Regulation 1

These Regulations may be cited as the Reporting of Injuries, Diseases and Dangerous Occurrences Regulations 1995 and shall come into force on 1 April 1996.

Regulation 2

Interpretation

Regulation 2

(1) In these Regulations, unless the context otherwise requires -

"the 1995 Order" means the Health and Safety at Work etc Act 1974 (Application Outside Great Britain) Order 1995;

"accident" includes

(a) an act of non-consensual physical violence done to a person at work; and

(b) an act of suicide which occurs on, or in the course of the operation of, a relevant transport system;

"approved" means approved for the time being in writing for the purposes of these Regulations by the Executive and published in such form as the Executive considers appropriate;

"biological agent" has the meaning assigned to it by regulation 2(1) of the Control of Substances Hazardous to Health Regulations 1994;

"construction site" means any place where there are carried out building operations or works of engineering construction such that those operations or works fall within section 127(1) of the Factories Act 1961;

"dangerous occurrence" means an occurrence which arises out of or in connection with work and is of a class specified in -

(a) paragraphs 1-17 of Part I of Schedule 2;

(b) paragraphs 18-21 of Part I of Schedule 2 and takes place elsewhere than at an offshore workplace;

(c) paragraphs 22-40 of Part II of Schedule 2 and takes place at a mine;

(d) paragraphs 41-48 of Part III of Schedule 2 and takes place at a quarry;

(e) paragraphs 49-72 of Part IV of Schedule 2 and takes place where a relevant transport system is operated (other than at a factory, dock, construction site, mine or quarry); or

(f) paragraphs 73-83 of Part V of Schedule 2 and takes place at an offshore workplace;

"disease" includes a medical condition;

"diving contractor" and "diving operation" have the meaning assigned to them by the Diving Operations at Work Regulations 1981;

"dock" means any place to which section 125(1) of the Factories Act 1961 applies;

Regulation

2

"the Executive" means the Health and Safety Executive;

"factory" has the meaning assigned to it by section 175 of the Factories Act 1961;

"guided transport system" means a system using a mode of guided transport prescribed under regulation 3 of the Railways and Other Transport Systems (Approval of Works, Plant and Equipment) Regulations 1994;

"major injury" means an injury or condition specified in Schedule 1;

"mine" or "quarry" means a mine or, as the case may be, a quarry within the meaning of section 180 of the Mines and Quarries Act 1954 and for the purposes of these Regulations includes a closed tip within the meaning of section 2(2)(b) of the Mines and Quarries (Tips) Act 1969 which is associated with that mine or that quarry;

"offshore installation" has the meaning assigned to it by article 4(2) of the 1995 Order but excluding the fixed structures specified in article 4(2)(a) of that Order;

"offshore workplace" means any place where activities are carried on or any premises such that prescribed provisions of the 1974 Act are applied to those activities or premises by virtue of articles 4, 5 or 6 of the 1995 Order, and for this purpose those articles shall be deemed to apply to activities or premises within Great Britain which are in tidal waters or on the foreshore or other land intermittently covered by such waters as they apply to activities and premises within territorial waters or a designated area;

"operator", in relation to a vehicle to which paragraph 16 or 17 of Part I of Schedule 2 applies, means -

(a) a person who holds an operator's licence (granted under Part V of the Transport Act 1968) for the use of that vehicle for the carriage of goods on a road; except that where by virtue of regulation 32(1) to (3) of the Goods Vehicles (Operators' Licences, Qualifications and Fees) Regulations 1984 the vehicle is included in a licence held by a holding company and that company is not operating the vehicle at the relevant time, the 'operator' shall be the subsidiary company specified in the application made under the said regulation 32(1) or, if more than one subsidiary company is so specified, whichever one is operating the vehicle at the relevant time, and in this sub-paragraph 'holding company' and 'subsidiary company' have the same meanings as in the said Regulations of 1984; or

(b) where no such licence is held -

(i) (in the case of a vehicle which is not registered in the United Kingdom) the driver of the vehicle, or

(ii) (in the case of any other vehicle) the keeper of the vehicle; and for this purpose, where the vehicle is on hire or lease to any person, that person shall be treated as its keeper;

but where an employee who would otherwise be the operator of a vehicle in accordance with sub-paragraph (b)(i) above uses that vehicle for the carriage of any dangerous substance on behalf of his employer, that employer shall (notwithstanding that sub-paragraph) be regarded as the operator of the vehicle concerned;

Regulation

2

"owner" means -

(a) in relation to a mine or quarry, the person who is for the time being entitled to work it;

(b) in relation to a pipeline, the person who is for the time being entitled to control the flow of anything through that pipeline or through that pipeline once it is commissioned;

"passenger train" means a train carrying passengers or made available for the carriage of passengers;

"pipeline" and "pipeline works" have the meaning assigned to them by article 6(2) of the 1995 Order;

"railway" has the meaning assigned to it by section 67 of the Transport and Works Act 1992;

"relevant transport system" means a railway, tramway, trolley vehicle system or guided transport system;

"responsible person" means -

(a) in the case of -

(i) a mine, the manager of that mine;

(ii) a quarry, the owner of that quarry;

(iii) a closed tip, the owner of the mine or quarry with which that tip is associated;

(iv) an offshore installation (otherwise than in the case of a disease reportable under regulation 5), the duty holder for the purposes of the Offshore Installations and Pipeline Works (Management and Administration) Regulations 1995 provided that for the purposes of this provision regulation 3(2)(c) of those Regulations shall be deemed not to apply;

(v) a dangerous occurrence at a pipeline (being an incident to which paragraph 14(a) - (f) of Part I of Schedule 2 applies), the owner of that pipeline;

(vi) a dangerous occurrence at a well , the person appointed by a concession owner to execute any function of organising or supervising any operation to be carried out by the well or, where no such person has been appointed, the concession owner (and for this purpose "concession owner" means the person who at any time has the right to exploit or explore mineral resources in any area, or to store gas in any area and to recover gas so stored if, at any time, the well is, or is to be, used in the exercise of that right);

(vii) a diving operation (otherwise than in the case of a disease reportable under regulation 5), the diving contractor;

(viii) a vehicle to which paragraph 16 or 17 of Part I of Schedule 2 applies, the operator of the vehicle;

Regulation

(b) (where sub-paragraph (a) above does not apply) in the case of the death of or other injury to an employee reportable under regulation 3 or of a disease suffered by an employee reportable under regulation 5, his employer; and

(c) in any other case, the person for the time being having control of the premises in connection with the carrying on by him of any trade, business or other undertaking (whether for profit or not) at which, or in connection with the work at which, the accident or dangerous occurrence reportable under regulation 3, or case of disease reportable under regulation 5, happened;

"road" has the meaning assigned to it by section 192(1) of the Road Traffic Act 1988;

"road vehicle" means any vehicle, other than a train, on a road;

"running line" means any line which is not a siding and is ordinarily used for the passage of trains;

"train" includes a reference to a locomotive, tramcar or other power unit and to a vehicle used on a relevant transport system;

"tramway" has the meaning assigned to it by section 67 of the Transport and Works Act 1992;

"trolley vehicle system" has the meaning assigned to it by section 67 of the Transport and Works Act 1992;

"well" includes any structures and devices on top of a well;

(2) In these Regulations, unless the context otherwise requires, any reference to -

(a) a numbered regulation or Schedule is a reference to the regulation or Schedule in these Regulations so numbered;

(b) a numbered paragraph is a reference to the paragraph so numbered in the regulation or Schedule in which that reference appears; and

(c) an accident or a dangerous occurrence which arises out of or in connection with work shall include a reference to an accident, or as the case may be, a dangerous occurrence attributable to the manner of conducting an undertaking, the plant or substances used for the purposes of an undertaking and the condition of the premises so used or any part of them.

(3) For the purposes of these Regulations, a person who is at an offshore workplace shall be deemed to be at work at all times when he is at that workplace in connection with his work.

2

Guide

Notes on selected definitions

Violence

14 'accident' has been defined as including 'an act of non consensual physical violence done to a person at work'. This has the effect of making injuries arising from such acts reportable if they fall into one of the categories in regulation 3(1)(a), 3(1)(b), 3(2) or 4.

2

Guide

15 The term 'non-consensual' is used to exclude injuries arising from situations where the injured person had agreed to the violent act taking place. This would exclude injuries arising from some work activities, particularly some types of professional sport, where taking part implies acceptance of a level of violence and risk of injury. For example, a major injury of the type reportable under regulation 3(1)(b) suffered by a professional sportsperson during the normal course of a game of rugby or a boxing match would not be regarded as an 'accident' for the purposes of these Regulations and would not need to be reported. A major injury suffered by a shop assistant assaulted by a customer or by a nurse assaulted by a patient in a psychiatric ward would be regarded as arising from an 'accident' and must be reported.

16 Only physical injuries resulting from acts of violence suffered by people who are at work are included in the definition of 'accident'. An act of violence done to a member of the public by, for example, an employee or another member of the public would not be regarded as an 'accident' for the purposes of these regulations and any resulting injury would not need to be reported.

17 Further guidance on the reporting of acts of violence is given at paragraph 37 under the guide on the definition of the phrase 'out of or in connection with work' under regulation 2(2).

18 Remember that incidents involving acts of violence may well need to be reported to the police, whether or not they are reportable to HSE or local authorities under these Regulations.

Offshore installation

19 This definition explains the use of the term 'offshore installation' in part (a)(iv) of the definition of 'responsible person' and in paragraphs 73 to 82 of Schedule 2 (dangerous occurrences reportable in respect of an offshore workstation). The full offshore scope of the Regulations is, however, wider than this (see 'offshore workplace' below and also regulation 12).

Offshore workplace

20 These Regulations apply to the offshore oil and gas industry (see regulation 12). Some provisions apply *only* offshore and these are identified by the term 'offshore workplace' (eg Schedule 2, part V, Schedule 3, part II and Schedule 6). The places and activities covered by these special provisions are:

- offshore installations and activities on them; most activities in connection with them; and certain diving activities;
- wells and most activities in connection with wells; and
- pipelines, pipeline works and certain activities in connection with pipeline works.

21 The term includes offshore installations, wells, pipelines and related activities in inshore tidal waters, but *not* those on land or in non-tidal waters such as lakes. It also excludes certain construction and other activities in territorial waters covered by articles 7 and 8 of the 1995 Order.

Operator of a vehicle

22 Dangerous occurrences involving the transport of dangerous goods by road are set out at paragraphs 16 and 17 of Schedule 2. If one of these takes place the

2

person who must notify and make a report to the enforcing authority is the 'operator' of the vehicle. The 'operator' is defined as being one of the following:

(a) a person who holds an operator's licence under Part V of the Transport Act 1968 to use the vehicle to transport goods on the road; or

(b) when the vehicle is included in a licence held by a holding company which is not operating it at the time and one or more subsidiary companies are covered by the licence, whichever subsidiary company is operating the vehicle; or

(c) if no operator's licence is held and the vehicle is not registered in the United Kingdom, the driver of the vehicle, unless the driver is an employee carrying dangerous substances on behalf of their employer, in which case the employer will be the 'operator'; or

(d) if no operator's licence is held and the vehicle is registered in the United Kingdom, the keeper of the vehicle, including anyone the vehicle is hired or leased to.

Pipelines and pipeline works

23 These definitions apply to both onshore and offshore pipelines, even though the 1995 Order only applies offshore.

Railways

24 The definitions of railway etc under 'relevant transport system' exclude those at factories, docks, construction sites, and at mines and quarries. As a result the dangerous occurrences in Part IV of Schedule 2 do not apply at those premises. Separate guidance is available on the application of these Regulations to relevant transport systems[2].

Responsible person

25 The 'responsible person' must notify, report and record the events (deaths, injuries and dangerous occurrences) which are covered by regulations 3 and 4 and the cases of disease covered by regulation 5.

26 Table 1 summarises who the responsible person is for all situations.

Self-employed people

27 As indicated in Table 1, when a self-employed person is injured or suffers ill health at work, whether they or someone else must report depends on who was in control of the premises where they were working at the time the injury or case of ill health occurred.

28 If, for example, a self-employed person is seriously injured while working for a firm of subcontractors on a large building site controlled by a main contractor, then the main contractor must report the injury. However, if the injured self-employed person is working in his or her own premises, or in other premises under his or her control at the time of the accident, then he or she must report the injury.

Table 1

Reportable event (under RIDDOR 1995)		*Responsible person*
1 **Special cases**		
All reportable events in mines		The mine manager
All reportable events in quarries or in closed mine or quarry tips		The owner
All reportable events at offshore installations, except cases of disease reportable under regulation 5		The owner, in respect of a mobile installation, or the operator in respect of a fixed installation (under these Regulations the responsibility extends to reporting incidents at subsea installations, except tied back wells and adjacent pipeline)
All reportable events at diving operations, except cases of disease reportable under regulation 5		The diving contractor
2 **Injuries and disease**		
Death, major injury, over-3-day injury, or case of disease (including cases of disease connected with diving operations and work at an offshore installation):	of an employee at work	That person's employer
	of a self-employed person at work in premises under the control of someone else	The person in control of the premises: ● at the time of the event; and ● in connection with their carrying on any trade, business or undertaking
Major injury, over-3-day injury, or case of disease:	of a self-employed person at work in premises under their control	The self-employed person or someone acting on their behalf
Death, or injury requiring removal to a hospital for treatment (or major injury occurring at a hospital):	of a person who is not at work (but is affected by the work of someone else), eg a member of the public, a student, a resident of a nursing home	The person in control of the premises where, or in connection with the work going on at which, the accident causing the injury happened: ● at the time of the event; and ● in connection with their carrying on any trade, business or undertaking

Table 1 (continued)

Reportable event (under RIDDOR 1995)	*Responsible person*
3 **Dangerous occurrences**	
One of the dangerous occurrences listed in Schedule 2 to the Regulations, except: ● where they occur at workplaces covered by part 1 of this table (ie at mines, quarries, closed mine or quarry tips, offshore installations or connected with diving operations); or ● those covered below (which are: paragraphs 13, 14(a) to (f), 16 and 17 of Schedule 2, Part I)	The person in control of the premises where, or in connection with the work going on at which, the dangerous occurrence happened: ● at the time the dangerous occurrence happened; and ● in connection with their carrying on any trade, business or undertaking
A dangerous occurrence at a well (see paragraph 13 of Schedule 2)	The concession owner (the person having the right to exploit or explore mineral resources and store and recover gas in any area, if the well is used or is to be used to exercise that right) or the person appointed by the concession owner to organise or supervise any operation carried out by the well
A dangerous occurrence at a pipeline (see paragraph 14(a) to (f) of Schedule 2), but not a dangerous occurrence connected with pipeline works (paragraph 14(g) of Schedule 2)	The owner of the pipeline
A dangerous occurrence involving a dangerous substance being conveyed by road (see paragraphs 16 and 17 of Schedule 2)	The operator of the vehicle

Guide

Peripatetic employees

29 Except in the 'special cases' listed in part 1 of Table 1 a reportable injury to a peripatetic employee (for example, a goods or postal delivery worker, a refuse collector, a sales representative, a building worker who travels from site to site, or a service engineer) must be reported by that person's employer, wherever the accident causing the injury happens. For example, if a peripatetic refrigeration engineer is seriously injured while working in a supermarket the engineer's employer must make the report, not the operator of the supermarket. Where a workplace is shared, co-operation between employers and self-employed people is required by regulation 9 of the Management of Health and Safety at Work Regulations 1992[3]. For that reason, an employer in control of premises where there is a reportable accident involving a peripatetic employee working away from base should inform that person's employer about it as soon as possible.

Informing the responsible person

30 To help responsible persons discharge their duties, employees need to be given clear guidelines about reporting accidents and cases of ill health to management. Internal reporting procedures need to ensure that prompt and clear information is given to the person within the organisation who is responsible for reporting to the enforcing authority.

Co-operation

31 The word 'premises' as defined by section 53 of the HSW Act has a very broad meaning. In some circumstances it can mean just part of a building or other workplace where the person in 'control' of that part may differ from the person in control in other areas, for example, part of an occupied factory building being demolished by a firm of demolition contractors. The boundaries between areas under different people's control may sometimes be difficult to determine, for example, in the case of a common access stairway in a building occupied by several employers. It is, therefore, important that those responsible for making reports in a given situation are identified through the arrangements for co-operation required under regulation 9 of the Management of Health and Safety at Work Regulations 1992[3] referred to earlier in this guidance.

Offshore installations

32 Item (a)(iv) under the definition of 'responsible person' makes the responsible person the owner, in respect of a mobile offshore installation, or the operator in respect of a fixed installation. These people are the 'duty holder' for the purposes of the Offshore Installations and Pipeline Works (Management and Administration) Regulations 1995 (MAR 1995). The definition in these Regulations, however, extends the duty holder's responsibilities to report incidents involving subsea installations (MAR 1995 does not apply to such installations). Tied back wells and the adjacent 500 m of pipeline are excluded (they are covered by (a)(v) and (vi) under the definition of 'responsible person').

Regulation 2(2)(c): 'Arising out of or in connection with work'

33 The phrase 'arising out of or in connection with work' is used in regulation 3(1). It defines the circumstances where that regulation applies and its meaning is therefore vital to understanding when the main accident

2

Guide

reporting requirements of these Regulations apply. For example, it is the key to determining whether or not accidents involving members of the public and others who are not at work at the time must be reported. It is also the key to determining whether or not accidents involving acts of violence between people who are at work must be reported.

34 Regulation 2(2)(c) directs that an accident or dangerous occurrence due to any of the following must be regarded as arising out of or in connection with work:

- 'the manner of conducting an undertaking'.

  This refers to the way in which any work activity is being carried out for the purposes of an undertaking, including how it is organised, supervised or performed by an employer or any of their employees, or by a self-employed person;

- 'the plant or substances used for the purposes of the undertaking'.

  This includes, for example: lifts; air conditioning plant; any machinery, equipment or appliance; gas installations; and substances used in connection with the premises or with processes carried on there;

- 'the condition of the premises used by the undertaking or of any part of them'.

  This includes the state of the structure or fabric of a building or outside area forming part of the premises and the state and design of floors, paving, stairs, lighting etc.

Effect of 'Arising out of or in connection with work' on reporting accidents involving people not at work

35 In the following examples the accidents, which involve people who are not at work, would all be regarded as arising out of or in connection with work. As a result, if one of the people died or suffered an injury leading to them being taken to a hospital for treatment, regulation 3(1)(c) would apply and the death or injury must be reported:

(a) someone shopping who was involved in an accident at an escalator in a shop, where the accident was attributable to the design or condition of the escalator;

(b) a patient/resident in a nursing or residential care home who tripped and fell over an obstruction such as an electrical cable lying across a floor in the home;

(c) a member of the public who, while visiting a factory, was overcome by fumes which escaped accidentally from a process being carried on there;

(d) a pupil or student, who was involved in an accident attributable in some way to:

    (i) work organisation (eg by a teacher);

    (ii) plant;

    (iii) a substance; or

    (iv) the condition of premises.

2

Guide

36 Similarly, If a patient in a hospital fell from a hospital window and broke a leg, the accident leading to the injury would be regarded as having arisen out of or in connection with work. Regulation 3(1)(d) would apply and the injury would have to be reported.

Effect of 'Arising out of or in connection with work' on reporting injuries arising from violence at work

37 If one of the people in the following examples died or suffered a major or over-3-day physical injury caused by a non-consensual act of physical violence while they were at work then regulation 3 would apply, meaning that the death or injury must be reported.

(a) an employee is hit by a supervisor while being given feedback on work performance;

(b) a supervisor is hit by an employee while giving an instruction to carry out a work-related task;

(c) a hospital porter is hit by a patient in an accident and emergency department;

(d) a new employee is injured while being forced to take part in an initiation ceremony.

38 Injuries suffered by the people in the following examples would not be regarded as arising out of or in connection with work and so would not have to be reported:

(a) an employee working on a factory production line hits another during an argument over a personal matter;

(b) an employee at work at a public enquiry desk is hit by one of his or her relatives who comes in to discuss a domestic matter.

39 Further guidance on reporting violent incidents is given in paragraph 14.

Regulation 2(3): Working offshore

40 Offshore workers are commonly accommodated offshore in between their work shifts. Injuries to workers while off-shift offshore are reportable in the same way as injuries during work shifts, as long as the injury results from an accident arising out of or in connection with work.

2

Regulation 3

Notification and reporting of injuries and dangerous occurrences

Regulation

(1) Subject to regulation 10, where -

(a) any person dies as a result of an accident arising out of or in connection with work;

(b) any person at work suffers a major injury as a result of an accident arising out of or in connection with work;

3

Regulation

(c) any person not at work suffers an injury as a result of an accident arising out of or in connection with work and that person is taken from the site of the accident to a hospital for treatment in respect of that injury;

(d) any person not at work suffers a major injury as a result of an accident arising out of or in connection with work at a hospital; or

(e) there is a dangerous occurrence,

the responsible person shall -

(i) forthwith notify the relevant enforcing authority thereof by the quickest practicable means; and

(ii) within 10 days send a report thereof to the relevant enforcing authority on a form approved for the purposes of this sub-paragraph, unless within that period he makes a report thereof to the Executive by some other means so approved.

(2) Subject to regulation 10, where a person at work is incapacitated for work of a kind which he might reasonably be expected to do, either under his contract of employment, or, if there is no such contract, in the normal course of his work, for more than three consecutive days (excluding the day of the accident but including any days which would not have been working days) because of an injury resulting from an accident arising out of or in connection with work (other than one reportable under paragraph (1)), the responsible person shall as soon as practicable and, in any event, within 10 days of the accident send a report thereof to the relevant enforcing authority on a form approved for the purposes of this regulation, unless within that period he makes a report thereof to the Executive by some other means so approved.

3

Guide

41 Regulation 3 sets out the requirements to notify and report certain deaths, injuries and dangerous occurrences. In order to understand the requirements it is important to appreciate the meaning of the key phrase 'arising out of or in connection with work', which is defined in regulation 2(2)(c), and the definitions of 'accident' and 'responsible person' in regulation 2(1).

42 The requirements of regulation 3 are subject to the restrictions set out in regulation 10.

Death

43 The death of any person, whether or not they are at work, must be reported if it results from an accident arising out of or in connection with work. Deaths of employees occurring some time after the accident are covered by regulation 4.

Major injury to a person at work

44 The reportable major injuries are set out in Schedule 1 to these Regulations.

Injuries to people not at work

45 Any injury to a person who is not at work (eg a hotel or care home resident, pupil or student, or a customer in a shop) must be reported if it:

3

Guide

(a) results from an accident arising out of or in connection with work; and

(b) results in them being taken from the premises where the accident occurred to a hospital, by whatever means (for example, by taxi, private car or ambulance), for treatment in respect of that injury.

46 Examples of reportable accidents involving people not at work are given in the guidance on regulation 2(2).

Injuries at a hospital to people not at work

47 If a person who is not at work is injured on hospital premises as a result of an accident arising out of or in connection with work the injury must be reported if it falls into one of the categories of major injury defined in Schedule 1 to these Regulations. The different requirements are designed to ensure the reporting of accidents at hospitals which would have required removal to a hospital if they had occurred elsewhere. Unlike other responsible persons, those at hospitals are more likely to be able to determine the precise nature of an injury to someone who is not at work.

Dangerous occurrences

48 The reportable dangerous occurrences are defined in Schedule 2 to these Regulations. If an injury occurs and is reportable under one of the other categories in regulation 3 then the dangerous occurrence should not be reported separately. If, however, the injury is not reportable under regulation 3 then the dangerous occurrence must be reported. Schedule 2 is divided into five parts: Part I contains a general list of dangerous occurrences, including a number not reportable in respect of offshore workplaces; Parts II, III, IV and V list dangerous occurrences which are specific to mines, quarries, relevant transport systems and offshore workplaces respectively.

Incidents on public roads

49 Only a limited number of accidents caused by moving vehicles on a public road are reportable (see regulation 10). However, when there has been a reportable injury or dangerous occurrence on the public road, it must still be reported under these Regulations even though it may already have been reported to or involved the police or other emergency services.

Notification and reporting

50 Regulation 3(1) lists the circumstances where the responsible person must:

(a) notify the enforcing authority by the quickest practicable means (but see the exclusion for the self-employed in regulation 10(5)); and then

(b) within 10 days of the accident happening make a report on an approved form or by some other means approved by the Health and Safety Executive.

51 In practice, notifying by the 'quickest practicable means' will normally mean a telephone call to the local office of the enforcing authority made during normal office hours. It is advisable to keep a note of telephone notifications, including the time, the name of the caller and what details were given of the event being notified.

3

Guide

52 'Forthwith' and 'within 10 days' refer to the time of the accident. However, there will be cases when the reportable injury or condition resulting from the accident will either:

(a) not be recognisable without a medical examination (eg a case of a fracture of the skull) which is conducted only after some delay; or

(b) be delayed for some time after the accident (eg some cases of acute illness where a substance has been absorbed).

In such cases the notification (and report) required by Regulation 3(1) should be made as soon as the injury or condition has been confirmed.

53 The approved form for making reports under regulation 3(1)(ii) and 3(2) is Form F2508. A sample copy of the form is reproduced at Appendix 2. Appendix 2 may be freely photocopied in order to make reports. However, pads of report forms are available from HSE Books[4]. A pack is also available from HSE Books containing report forms on floppy disk together with a copy of this guide[5]. Separate forms must be used to report offshore incidents (OIR/9B). These are available from the HSE Offshore Safety Division offices listed at Appendix 1.

54 The phrase 'unless within that period he makes a report thereof to the Executive by some other means so approved' allows the Health and Safety Executive to approve systems of reporting other than sending a written form. This would allow the Executive, for example, to approve reporting by telephone alone. Pilot trials are being undertaken in 1996 to evaluate telephone only reporting systems. If the Executive approved any such system in the future the change would be widely publicised.

Over-3-day injuries

55 Regulation 3(2) only applies to injuries resulting from accidents to people who are at work and to injuries which are not reportable under regulation 3(1).

56 A report must be sent to the enforcing authority if the injured person is incapacitated for work for more than three consecutive days, not counting the day of the accident but including any days which would not have been working days. The expression 'more than three consecutive days' means, in practice, at least four days. For example, if a person who normally works Monday to Friday is injured on Friday and returns to work the following Wednesday, the Saturday and Sunday would have to be included when counting the days of incapacity. The total period of incapacity would be four days and the injury must be reported.

57 The regulation is not confined to cases of incapacity which keep injured people away from work. For example, if an injured employee turns up for work immediately following an accident and is, for more than three days, put on light duties which are not part of their normal work (a skilled machinist put on light cleaning duties, perhaps), then the injury must be reported.

Reporting to the enforcing authority

58 In all of the above cases, and in the case of regulations 4, 5, and 6, notification and reports must be made to the relevant enforcing authority. This is the body responsible for enforcing the HSW Act (and other relevant statutory provisions) in the premises where, or in connection with the work at which, the reportable event happened. In the case of regulation 6 the enforcing authority is HSE. In other situations the enforcing authority may be HSE, or a local authority.

Guide

3

59 Telephone notifications and reports should be made to the appropriate HSE Area office or specialist division or inspectorate, as set out in Appendix 1 or to the office of the relevant local authority.

60 The split of enforcement responsibility between HSE and local authorities is determined by the Health and Safety (Enforcing Authority) Regulations 1989. In summary, however, local authorities are responsible for enforcing health and safety legislation in:

- retailing;
- some warehouses;
- most offices;
- hotels and catering;
- sports;
- leisure;
- consumer services; and
- places of worship.

Regulation 4

Reporting of the death of an employee

Regulation

4

Subject to regulation 10, where an employee, as a result of an accident at work, has suffered an injury reportable under regulation 3 which is a cause of his death within one year of the date of that accident, the employer shall inform the relevant enforcing authority in writing of the death as soon as it comes to his knowledge, whether or not the accident has been reported under regulation 3.

Guide

4

61 The requirements in regulation 3(1) to report fatalities are intended to apply in practice to any death which occurs at the time of an accident or within a few days. Whether or not deaths which occur after longer delays must be reported depends on the nature of the initial injuries and on whether or not the injured person was an employee at work at the time of the accident.

62 Regulation 4 requires that if an employee dies after some delay as a result of suffering at work an injury or condition which is reportable under regulation 3, then the employer must inform the enforcing authority about the death in writing, provided that it occurs within a year of the date of the accident. This must be done whether or not the original injury had been reported.

63 Regulation 4 only applies to employees. The death is not reportable if someone other than an employee (for example, a pupil at school or a pedestrian near a building site) subsequently dies from an injury of the type reportable under regulation 3(1)(c) or 3(1)(d) suffered as a result of an accident arising out of or in connection with the work activity of someone else.

Regulation 5

Reporting of cases of disease

Regulation

(1) Subject to paragraphs (2) and (3) and to regulation 10, where -

(a) a person at work suffers from any of the occupational diseases specified in column 1 of Part I of Schedule 3 and his work involves one of the activities specified in the corresponding entry in column 2 of that Part; or

(b) a person at an offshore workplace suffers from any of the diseases specified in Part II of Schedule 3,

the responsible person shall forthwith send a report thereof to the relevant enforcing authority on a form approved for the purposes of this regulation, unless he forthwith makes a report thereof to the Executive by some other means so approved.

(2) Paragraph (1) shall apply only if -

(a) in the case of an employee, the responsible person has received a written statement prepared by a registered medical practitioner diagnosing the disease as one of those specified in Schedule 3;or

(b) in the case of a self-employed person, that person has been informed, by a registered medical practitioner, that he is suffering from a disease so specified.

(3) In the case of a self-employed person, it shall be a sufficient compliance with paragraph (1) if that person makes arrangements for the report to be sent to the relevant enforcing authority by some other person.

5

Guide

64 The requirements of regulation 5 are subject to the restrictions set out in regulation 10.

65 Regulation 5 requires employers and self-employed people to report cases of certain diseases which are linked with specified work activities and, in the case of offshore workers, certain other diseases. The reportable diseases and corresponding work activities, together with those additionally reportable offshore, are set out in Schedule 3 to these Regulations.

When to report

66 Under Regulation 5, the responsible person must make a report if:

(a) they receive, in respect of an employee, a written diagnosis of one of the occupational diseases in column 1 of Schedule 3, Part I (for example, on a medical certificate) made out by a doctor; and

(b) the ill employee's current job involves the corresponding work activity specified in column 2 of Part 1 of the Schedule.

67 In addition, where the employee was at an offshore workplace an employer must also make a report if they receive, in respect of an employee, a written diagnosis of one of the diseases listed in Part II of Schedule 3, made out by a doctor.

68 When employers receive written statements by doctors they should check against Schedule 3 whether reports must be made. They can simplify this job by identifying which of their work activities are covered by Column 2 of Schedule 3, Part I and then short-listing those diseases in Column 1 which they

5

Guide

might need to report. In doing this, employers can usefully draw on the list of hazards identified and recorded as part of their duty under the Management of Health and Safety at Work Regulations 1992[3] to carry out a risk assessment. Additional guidance on certain of the conditions listed in Schedule 3, Part I is provided in the table annexed to the Schedule.

The self-employed

69 For self-employed people the basis for reporting is slightly different as they do not normally need written statements from their doctors when off work through illness. To take account of this, a written statement is not required to trigger a report. If a self-employed person is diagnosed by a doctor to be suffering from one of the diseases in Schedule 3, and is told about it directly by the doctor, then they (or someone on their behalf) must report it. As with employees, this only applies if their current job involves the corresponding work activity specified in the Schedule (unless they are at an offshore workplace and a disease from Part II of the Schedule is being reported).

Making a report

70 The approved form for making reports under regulation 5 is Form F2508A. A sample copy of the form is reproduced at Appendix 2. Appendix 2 may be freely photocopied in order to make reports. However, pads of report forms are available from HSE Books[4]. A pack is also available from HSE Books containing RIDDOR report forms on floppy disk together with a copy of this guidance[5]. The report must be made to the appropriate enforcing authority, as set out in the guidance under regulation 3. A record of the report must also be kept as set out in the guidance on regulation 7.

71 The phrase in regulation 5(1) 'unless within that period he makes a report thereof to the Executive by some other means so approved' allows the Health and Safety Executive to approve systems of reporting other than sending a written form. This would allow the Executive, for example, to approve reporting by telephone alone. If the Executive approved any such system in the future the change would be widely publicised.

The role of doctors

72 Doctors are encouraged to use standard wording when describing reportable diseases on written statements which they make out for their patients.

73 The HSE's interest in occupational ill health goes wider than the gathering of information under these Regulations and the diseases covered by them. The Employment Medical Advisory Service (EMAS) will continue to be available to give advice on any occupational health problem, whether suspected by the employer or diagnosed by a doctor. Employers and employees can seek advice from EMAS about the reportable diseases or any other disease.

5

Regulation 6

Reporting of gas incidents

Regulation

(1) Whenever a conveyor of flammable gas through a fixed pipe distribution system, or a filler, importer or supplier (other than by means of retail trade) of a refillable container containing liquefied petroleum gas receives notification of any death or any major injury which has arisen out of or in connection with the gas distributed, filled, imported or supplied, as the case may be, by that person, he shall forthwith notify the Executive of the incident, and shall within 14 days send a report of it to the Executive on a form approved for the purposes of this regulation.

6

Regulation

(2) Whenever an employer or self-employed person who is a member of a class of persons approved by the Executive for the purposes of paragraph (3) of regulation 3 of the Gas Safety (Installation and Use) Regulations 1994 has in his possession sufficient information for it to be reasonable for him to decide that a gas fitting as defined in the said Regulations or any flue or ventilation used in connection with that fitting, by reason of its design, construction, manner of installation, modification or servicing, is or has been likely to cause death, or any major injury by reason of -

(a) accidental leakage of gas;

(b) inadequate combustion of gas; or

(c) inadequate removal of the products of combustion of gas,
he shall within 14 days send a report of it to the Executive on a form approved for the purposes of this regulation, unless he has previously reported such information.

(3) Nothing shall be reportable -

(a) under this regulation if it is notifiable or reportable elsewhere in these Regulations;

(b) under paragraph (2) in relation to any gas fitting, flue or ventilation undergoing testing or examination at a place set aside for that purpose.

(4) In this regulation "liquefied petroleum gas" means commercial butane (that is, a hydrocarbon mixture consisting predominantly of butane, butylene or any mixture thereof) or commercial propane (that is, a hydrocarbon mixture consisting predominantly of propane, propylene or any mixture thereof) or any mixture of commercial butane and commercial propane.

6

Guide

Regulation 6(1): Gas incident causing death or injury

74 The trigger for a report to the HSE under regulation 6(1) is the receipt by the person on whom the reporting duty is placed of 'notification' of a flammable gas incident causing a death or a major injury other than one reportable under regulation 3(1). Neither the method nor source of this 'notification' is specified. It may be advice or information about the occurrence of the incident in writing, by telephone or through the press, radio or television. It may come, for example, from an employee or other person engaged in gas installation or servicing work, a retailer of refillable Liquefied Petroleum Gas (LPG) containers, a householder or other customer, a police officer, a member of the fire service, or from any other person.

75 In the case of a reportable incident involving LPG in a refillable container, the person who must make a report to the HSE will be any of the following who received notification in any of the ways described in the previous paragraph:

(a) if the container was filled abroad, the importer of the gas-filled container, if it was of foreign origin;

(b) the filler of the container;

(c) the wholesaler or other supplier (but not retailer) of the gas-filled container.

76 Under both regulation 6(1) and 6(2) reports of gas incidents and dangerous gas fittings need to be made for all those involving the use of either mains gas or LPG from bulk tanks or cylinders.

6

Guide

Regulation 6(2): Gas fittings found to be dangerous

77 Regulation 6(2) deals with gas fittings and associated flue and ventilation arrangements used in connection with flammable gas supplied through fixed pipe distribution systems. The gas fittings which are covered are those defined by the Gas Safety (Installation and Use) Regulations 1994, ie gas pipes, fittings, meters, apparatus and appliances designed for use by consumers of gas for lighting, heating, motive power and other purposes for which flammable gases can be used. The regulation covers all commonly used fuel gases, ie natural gas and LPG (propane and butane).

78 Whether or not a registered installation business makes a report about a particular situation, under regulation 6(2), depends on their making a judgement. This will be based on information in their possession and in the light of their own knowledge and experience, about two matters relating to that situation:

(a) whether there is or has been a design, construction, installation, modification or servicing fault in a gas fitting or associated flue or ventilation arrangement which has resulted or is likely to result in:

  (i) an accidental leakage of the gas; or

  (ii) inadequate combustion of the gas; or

  (iii) inadequate removal of the products of combustion of the gas; but only if

(b) the resulting leakage, inadequate combustion or inadequate removal of the products of combustion is or has been likely to cause death or a major injury.

79 In the case of gas leaks attributable to installation faults, the gas installer's judgement about (b) above would have to take into account whether or not the leak was likely to lead to a fire or explosion. In any circumstances where the gas installer considers it necessary to disconnect any part of the installation to avert danger, a report would normally be needed.

80 However, it should be noted that regulation 6(2) does not apply in addition to the requirements of regulation 6(1) or regulation 3(1) : ie. where someone dies or suffers a major injury as a result of a flammable gas incident, or where there is a dangerous occurrence involving flammable gas.

81 The following are examples of the kinds of fault described in paragraph 78(a) which, if likely to cause death or a major injury, would be reportable under regulation 6(2):

(a) a dangerous gas leak arising, for example, from the use of unsatisfactory materials or bad workmanship;

(b) a gas appliance which for any reason is spilling its products of combustion;

(c) a gas appliance which shows clear signs of incomplete combustion;

(d) a gas appliance which shows signs of combustion problems due to inadequate provisions for ventilation;

6

Guide

(e) a gas appliance which is not suitable for use with the gas supplied;

(f) a gas appliance in use on which a safety device such as a flame-failure device has been made inoperative;

(g) an appliance which is connected to the gas supply by a flexible connection made of an unsatisfactory material, such as a garden hose;

(h) an appliance or installation which has become, or remains, dangerous because of faulty servicing.

82 If any of these faults have actually caused death or a major injury, they should be reported under Regulation 6(1).

Reporting a gas incident

83 Reports of gas incidents must be made to the relevant HSE Area Office using the report form F2508G. These forms are available from HSE Books. Registered gas installers can also obtain the form from the Council of Registered Gas Installers (CORGI).

6

Regulation 7 Records

Regulation

(1) The responsible person shall keep a record of -

(a) any event which is required to be reported under regulation 3, which shall contain the particulars specified in Part I of Schedule 4;

(b) any case of disease required to be reported under regulation 5(1), which shall contain the particulars specified in Part II of Schedule 4; and

(c) such other particulars as may be approved by the Executive for the purpose of demonstrating that any approved means of reporting under regulations 3 or 5(1) has been complied with.

(2) Any record of deaths, injuries at work or disease which the responsible person keeps for any other purpose shall, if it covers the injuries recordable under these Regulations and includes the particulars specified in Schedule 4, be sufficient for the requirements of paragraph (1).

(3) The record referred to in paragraph (1) shall be kept either at the place where the work to which it relates is carried on or at the usual place of business of the responsible person and an entry in such a record shall be kept for at least three years from the date on which it was made.

(4) The responsible person shall send to the relevant enforcing authority such extracts from the record required to be kept under paragraph (1) as that enforcing authority may from time to time require.

7

Guide

84 The responsible person is required to keep records of every event which must be reported under regulations 3 and 5. The details to be included in each record are set out in Schedule 4 to these Regulations.

85 The Health and Safety Executive is given the power to require a record to be kept to demonstrate that a report has been made. This power would be used if a non paper based reporting system, such as reporting by telephone only, was approved by the Executive using the powers in regulations 3 and 5. If the Executive were to approve any such system in the future the change would be widely publicised.

7

Guide

7

Ways of making and keeping records

86 Records must contain the details set out in Schedule 4, but their design and nature are not specified. Regulation 7 allows flexibility in the way records are made and kept and enables employers to choose arrangements which suit their own needs. Records kept for other purposes will satisfy the requirements as long as they contain the details in Schedule 4. For example, to record reportable events an employer could choose:

(a) in the case of accidents and diseases to keep photocopies of completed Forms F2508 and F2508A in a file or folder. One advantage of this could be that a good deal more detailed information may be kept than otherwise might be the case and the design of the form may provide a useful basis for the analysis of the collected data; or

(b) to store the information about each accident and reported case of disease on a computer: this would be acceptable provided that details from the computer file could be retrieved and printed out readily when required;

(c) in the case of accidents, to utilise the BI510 Accident Book which must be kept by certain employers under the Social Security (Claims and Payments) Regulations 1979. In this case they should use a suitable method of identifying which of the accidents recorded in the book are reportable under RIDDOR 1995 (as this method only covers accidents a separate method, for example (a) or (b) would need to be chosen to record reported cases of disease).

Location of records

87 The records must be kept either where the work to which they relate is carried out or at the usual place of business of the responsible person. For example, a retail chain may have a system in place where a safety officer makes reports to the enforcing authorities from a central point. In such a case the records may be kept either at the individual shops where the work to which they relate takes place, or at the offices of the safety officer. Records of offshore incidents would normally be kept at a suitable place onshore.

Making records available

88 Extracts from the records must be sent to the enforcing authority on request. In addition, using powers under Section 20 of HSW Act, an inspector from the enforcing authority may require any part of the records to be produced. If such a request is made the records should be produced as soon as possible. In practice, the time taken to produce the records will depend on whether or not they are kept at the place where the work is done or, where applicable, held centrally at the offices of the responsible person.

89 The Safety Representatives and Safety Committees Regulations 1977[6] require employers to make relevant health and safety documents available to safety representatives. This would include records kept under RIDDOR, except for records which reveal personal health information about identifiable people (see also regulation 8 and Schedule 5 on the powers of 'nominated persons' in mines).

Use of records

90 One aim of the record-keeping provisions of regulation 7 is to ensure that employers collect a minimum amount of data on health and safety incidents

Guide

7

connected with their undertaking, so that they can analyse these for performance monitoring and other safety management purposes. Some employers, often in conjunction with safety committees, find it advantageous to gather and analyse information on a wider range of incidents than just those which have to be reported under these Regulations. Such information is a valuable health and safety management tool and can be used as an aid to risk assessment and in developing strategies to help prevent accidents and ill health and to control costs imposed by accidental loss.

Regulation 8

Additional provisions relating to mines and quarries

Regulation 8

The provisions of Schedule 5 (which contains additional provisions relating to mines and quarries) shall have effect.

Regulation 9

Additional provisions relating to offshore workplaces

Regulation 9

The provisions of Schedule 6 (which contains additional provisions relating to offshore workplaces) shall have effect.

Regulation 10

Restrictions on the application of regulations 3, 4 and 5

Regulation 10

(1) The requirements of regulation 3 relating to the death or injury of a person as a result of an accident shall not apply to an accident causing death or injury to a person arising out of the conduct of any operation on, or any examination or other medical treatment of, that person which is administered by, or conducted under the supervision of, a registered medical practitioner or a registered dentist (and for the purposes of this paragraph a registered dentist has the meaning assigned to it by section 53(1) of the Dentists Act 1984).

(2) The requirements of regulations 3 and 4 relating to the death or injury of a person as a result of an accident, shall apply to an accident arising out of or in connection with the movement of a vehicle on a road only if that person -

(a) was killed or suffered an injury as a result of exposure to a substance being conveyed by the vehicle; or

(b) was either himself engaged in, or was killed or suffered an injury as a result of the activities of another person who was at the time of the accident engaged in, work connected with the loading or unloading of any article or substance onto or off the vehicle; or

(c) was either himself engaged in, or was killed or suffered an injury as a result of the activities of another person who was at the time of the accident engaged in, work on or alongside a road, being work concerned with the construction, demolition, alteration, repair or maintenance of -

(i) the road or the markings or equipment thereon;

(ii) the verges, fences, hedges or other boundaries of the road;

Regulation

(iii) pipes or cables on, under, over or adjacent to the road; or

(iv) buildings or structures adjacent to or over the road; or

(d) was killed or suffered an injury as a result of an accident involving a train.

(3) The requirements of regulations 3, 4 and 5 relating to any death, injury or case of disease shall not apply to a member of the armed forces of the Crown or of a visiting force who was on duty at the relevant time (and for the purposes of this paragraph a visiting force has the meaning assigned to it by section 12(1) of the Visiting Forces Act 1952).

(4) Regulations 3, 4 and 5 shall not apply otherwise than in respect of offshore workplaces to anything which is required to be notified under any of the enactments or instruments specified in Schedule 7.

(5) Regulation 3(1)(i) shall not apply to a self-employed person who is injured at premises of which he is the owner or occupier, but regulation 3(1)(ii) shall apply to such a self-employed person (other than in the case of death) and it shall be sufficient compliance with that sub-paragraph if that self-employed person makes arrangements for the report to be sent to the relevant enforcing authority by some other person.

10

Guide

Injury under medical supervision

91 If a person is injured as a result of an accident arising directly from the conduct of the specified medical procedures being carried out by or under the supervision of a registered medical practitioner or dentist, then the injury does not need to be reported. The exclusion does not extend to injuries arising from accidents to patients occurring under any other circumstances. For example, if a patient died or suffered a major injury as a result of a power failure during an operation (and not caused by the conduct of the operation) the death or injury must be reported.

Accidents caused by moving vehicles on the road

92 Regulations 3 and 4 do not apply to accidents involving vehicles moving on public roads unless they involve or are connected with:

(a) exposure to any substance being conveyed by road;

(b) vehicle loading and unloading activities such as those engaged in by refuse collectors, brewery delivery workers, furniture removers, etc;

(c) the specified construction, demolition, alteration, repair or maintenance activities on or alongside public roads; or

(d) an accident involving a train where a person is killed or injured.

93 In the case of (a) to (c) in paragraph 92 regulations 3 and 4 apply whether the injured person is engaged in one of the listed activities or whether they are injured as a result of the work of someone else who is engaged in such activities. For example, the following would be reportable under regulation 3:

(a) an employee of a building materials supplier dies as a result of being struck by a passing car while unloading bricks from a lorry;

(b) a motorist, who is not at work, driving past a building site alongside the road is injured and taken to hospital as a result of an accident caused by the car being hit by falling scaffolding from the site;

10

Guide

(c) the driver of a road tanker suffers gassing and acute illness as a result of exposure to a toxic substance spilled from the tanker, or, as a result of the same spillage a member of the public is taken to hospital for treatment as a result of exposure to the substance;

(d) an employee painting road markings is hit by a car and does not suffer a major injury as a result, but is unable to do his or her normal work for four days.

94 Dangerous occurrences on public highways are covered by the Regulations, and so too are accidents and dangerous occurrences on private roads (ie those not covered by the Road Traffic Act 1988).

Avoiding dual reporting

95 Except in the case of offshore workplaces (where HSE needs immediate information about incidents involving offshore installations or pipelines and shipping or aircraft) regulations 3, 4 and 5 do not apply to any of the events reportable under the Acts and Statutory Instruments listed in Schedule 7. This means that these Regulations do not apply to:

(a) a death or injury associated with the operation of a civil aircraft between the time anyone boards it with the intention of flight and the time everyone has subsequently disembarked;

(b) the death or injury of anyone employed on, or carried in, a merchant ship (unless that person is a shore-based worker involved in loading, unloading, repair work, etc);

(c) the death or injury of anyone as a result of an accidental explosion or fire in or about premises to which the Explosives Act 1875 applies;

(d) any incident involving the escape from control of a radioactive substance;

(e) any dangerous occurrence on board a merchant ship.

Self-employed people

96 If a self-employed person suffers a major injury while working at their own premises they do not have to notify the enforcing authority immediately, as normally required by regulation 3(1)(i) . The requirement at regulation 3(ii) to report within 10 days still applies, but self-employed people are allowed to make arrangements for someone else to report such injuries on their behalf.

10

Regulation 11

Defence in proceedings for an offence contravening these Regulations

Regulation 11

It shall be a defence in proceedings against any person for an offence under these Regulations for that person to prove that he was not aware of the event requiring him to notify or send a report to the relevant enforcing authority and that he had taken all reasonable steps to have all such events brought to his notice.

Regulation 12

Extension outside Great Britain

Regulation

12

These Regulations shall apply to and in relation to the premises and activities outside Great Britain to which sections 1 to 59 and 80 to 82 of the Health and Safety at Work etc Act 1974 apply by virtue of the 1995 Order as they apply within Great Britain.

Guide

12

97 The Regulations apply to certain work activities carried out in United Kingdom territorial waters adjacent to Great Britain and in the United Kingdom sector of the Continental Shelf . These are the work activities specified by the Health and Safety at Work etc Act 1974 (Application outside Great Britain) Order 1995, which include for example: offshore installations; wells; pipelines and pipeline works; and related activities. The Regulations also apply to mines under the sea and certain other activities in territorial waters, such as: the loading and unloading of ships; the construction and repair of ships; the construction and repair of buildings or other structures; and certain diving operations.

Regulation 13

Certificates of exemption

Regulation

13

(1) Subject to paragraph (2) and to any of the provisions imposed by the Communities in respect of the encouragement of improvements in the safety and health of workers at work, the Executive may, by a certificate in writing, exempt any person or class of persons from any requirement imposed by these Regulations and any such exemption may be granted subject to conditions and with or without limit of time and may be revoked by a certificate in writing at any time.

(2) The Executive shall not grant any such exemption unless, having regard to the circumstances of the case and, in particular, to -

(a) the conditions, if any, which it proposes to attach to the exemption; and

(b) any other requirements imposed by or under any enactments which apply to the case,

it is satisfied that the health and safety of persons who are likely to be affected by the exemption will not be prejudiced in consequence of it.

Guide

13

98 Regulation 13 gives the Health and Safety Executive limited power to grant exemptions to the requirements of these Regulations. Exemptions can only be granted where the provisions of European legislation allow and where the Executive is satisfied that the health and safety of any people likely to be affected by them will not be adversely affected.

Regulation 14

Repeal and amendment of provisions in the Regulation of Railways Act 1871, the Railway Employment (Prevention of Accidents) Act 1900 and the Transport and Works Act 1992

Regulation

14

(1) Section 6 (Companies to make returns of accidents to Board of Trade) of the Regulation of Railways Act 1871 section 13(2) of the Railway Employment (Prevention of Accidents) Act 1900 and sections 43 (Accidents etc.) and 44 (Accidents etc: consequential amendments) of the Transport and Works Act 1992 are hereby repealed.

Regulation

14

(2) The Regulation of Railways Act 1871 shall be amended as follows -

(a) in section 2 (Interpretation) there shall be added at the end the words "The term 'relevant transport system' has the meaning assigned to it by regulation 2 of the Reporting of Injuries, Diseases and Dangerous Occurrences Regulations 1995.";

(b) in section 7 (Inquiry into accidents and formal investigation in serious cases) for the words "accident, of which notice is for the time being required by or in pursuance of this Act to be sent to the Board of Trade" there shall be substituted the words " accident or occurrence which arises from the operation of a relevant transport system and which is required to be reported by regulation 3(1) of the Reporting of Injuries, Diseases and Dangerous Occurrences Regulations 1995";

(c) in section 7, after the word "accident", in each place where it subsequently occurs, there shall be added the words "or occurrence";

(d) in section 8 (Appointment of an assessor to coroner) for the words "accident, of which notice for the time being is required by or in pursuance of this Act to be sent to the Board of Trade" there shall be substituted the words "accident or occurrence-

(a) which arises from the operation of a relevant transport system, and

(b) which is required to be reported under regulation 3(1) of the Reporting of Injuries, Diseases and Dangerous Occurrences Regulations 1995,"; and

(e) in section 8, after the word "accident", in the second place where it occurs, there shall be inserted the words "or occurrence".

Regulation 15 Revocations, amendments and savings

Regulation

15

(1) The instruments specified in column 1 of Part I of Schedule 8 are hereby revoked to the extent specified in the corresponding entries in column 3 of that Part.

(2) The instruments specified in Part II of Schedule 8 are hereby amended to the extent specified in that Part.

(3) Any record or register required to be kept under any instrument revoked by these Regulations, shall be kept in the same manner and for the same period as if these Regulations had not been made.

Schedule 1

Major Injuries

Regulation 2(1)

Schedule

1 Any fracture, other than to the fingers, thumbs or toes.

2 Any amputation.

3 Dislocation of the shoulder, hip, knee or spine.

4 Loss of sight (whether temporary or permanent).

5 A chemical or hot metal burn to the eye or any penetrating injury to the eye.

6 Any injury resulting from an electric shock or electrical burn (including any electrical burn caused by arcing or arcing products) leading to unconsciousness or requiring resuscitation or admittance to hospital for more than 24 hours.

7 Any other injury -

(a) leading to hypothermia, heat-induced illness or to unconsciousness,

(b) requiring resuscitation, or

(c) requiring admittance to hospital for more than 24 hours.

8 Loss of consciousness caused by asphyxia or by exposure to a harmful substance or biological agent.

9 Either of the following conditions which result from the absorption of any substance by inhalation, ingestion or through the skin -

(a) acute illness requiring medical treatment; or

(b) loss of consciousness.

10 Acute illness which requires medical treatment where there is reason to believe that this resulted from exposure to a biological agent or its toxins or infected material.

1

Guide

99 The following notes explain some of the main terms used:

(a) *fracture* includes a break, crack or chip;

(b) *amputation* means either traumatic amputation at the time of the accident or surgical amputation following the accident (but the latter is more likely to be covered by 7(c));

(c) *requiring admittance to hospital for more than 24 hours* includes situations where, had the injured person not already been in hospital, the injury would have resulted in admission for more than 24 hours;

(d) *acute illness* means illness which:

(i) progresses rapidly to a crisis after the onset of symptoms: and

(ii) has severe symptoms;

Schedule 1

Guide

(e) *medical treatment* covers hospital treatment, treatment by a general medical practitioner, or treatment by a firm's medical and nursing staff;

(f) *loss of consciousness* means the injured person enters into a state, for however short a period, where there is a lack of response, either vocal or physical, to people trying to communicate with them;

(g) *biological agent* is defined in the Control of Substances Hazardous to Health Regulations 1994 as meaning 'any micro-organism, cell culture, or human endoparasite including any which have been genetically modified, which may cause any infection, allergy, toxicity or otherwise create a risk to human health'. In the context of the infection hazards relevant to RIDDOR 1995 this will in practice cover bacteria, viruses, fungi and parasites.

100 The following notes indicate the kinds of accidents which can lead to the reportable health conditions included in the list of major injuries:

(a) loss of consciousness resulting from asphyxia (lack of oxygen):

  (i) entry of a person into a confined space containing an oxygen deficient atmosphere;

  (ii) failure of air or oxygen supply in breathing apparatus;

(b) acute illness (absorption of any substance):

  (i) overturning, collapse or bursting of something containing a toxic substance, causing a spillage which contaminates the working environment;

  (ii) handling of surfaces of plant, containers etc, onto which a skin absorbable toxic substance had leaked without the knowledge of the person affected;

  (iii) use or handling of material containing a toxic substance, the presence of which was not known, in a way which led to an episode of high exposure to that substance;

  (iv) an unexpected reaction between chemical compounds giving off a toxic gas or vapour which contaminates the working environment;

  (v) inadvertent or unknowing entry of a person into a confined space containing a toxic gas or vapour;

(c) acute illness (exposure to a biological agent or its toxins or infected material):

  (i) escape or release of a biological agent or its toxins or infected material into a working environment by, for example, the failure of a fermenter or a centrifuge, breakage of a flask, a spillage, filter failure;

  (ii) exposure to a biological agent or its toxins or infected material through, for example, accidental self-inoculation (eg by the needle of a syringe or other contaminated sharp item), animal bite or laceration.

Schedule 1

Schedule 2

Dangerous occurrences

Regulation 2(1)

Schedule

Part I General

Lifting machinery, etc

1 The collapse of, the overturning of, or the failure of any load-bearing part of any -

(a) lift or hoist;

(b) crane or derrick;

(c) mobile powered access platform;

(d) access cradle or window-cleaning cradle;

(e) excavator;

(f) pile-driving frame or rig having an overall height, when operating, of more than 7 metres; or

(g) fork lift truck.

Pressure systems

2 The failure of any closed vessel (including a boiler or boiler tube) or of any associated pipework, in which the internal pressure was above or below atmospheric pressure, where the failure has the potential to cause the death of any person.

Freight containers

3 (1) The failure of any freight container in any of its load-bearing parts while it is being raised, lowered or suspended.

(2) In this paragraph, "freight container" means a container as defined in regulation 2(1) of the Freight Containers (Safety Convention) Regulations 1984.

Overhead electric lines

4 Any unintentional incident in which plant or equipment either -

(a) comes into contact with an uninsulated overhead electric line in which the voltage exceeds 200 volts; or

(b) causes an electrical discharge from such an electric line by coming into close proximity to it.

Electrical short circuit

5 Electrical short circuit or overload attended by fire or explosion which results in the stoppage of the plant involved for more than 24 hours or which has the potential to cause the death of any person.

2, Part I

Schedule

2, Part I

Explosives

6 (1) Any of the following incidents involving explosives -

(a) the unintentional explosion or ignition of explosives other than one -

(i) caused by the unintentional discharge of a weapon where, apart from that unintentional discharge, the weapon and explosives functioned as they were designed to do; or

(ii) where a fail-safe device or safe system of work functioned so as to prevent any person from being injured in consequence of the explosion or ignition;

(b) a misfire (other than one at a mine or quarry or inside a well or one involving a weapon) except where a fail-safe device or safe system of work functioned so as to prevent any person from being endangered in consequence of the misfire;

(c) the failure of the shots in any demolition operation to cause the intended extent of collapse or direction of fall of a building or structure;

(d) the projection of material (other than at a quarry) beyond the boundary of the site on which the explosives are being used or beyond the danger zone in circumstances such that any person was or might have been injured thereby;

(e) any injury to a person (other than at a mine or quarry or one otherwise reportable under these Regulations) involving first-aid or medical treatment resulting from the explosion or discharge of any explosives or detonator.

(2) In this paragraph "explosives" means any explosive of a type which would, were it being transported, be assigned to Class 1 within the meaning of the Classification and Labelling of Explosives Regulations 1983 and "danger zone" means the area from which persons have been excluded or forbidden to enter to avoid being endangered by any explosion or ignition of explosives.

Biological agents

7 Any accident or incident which resulted or could have resulted in the release or escape of a biological agent likely to cause severe human infection or illness.

Malfunction of radiation generators, etc

8 (1) Any incident in which -

(a) the malfunction of a radiation generator or its ancillary equipment used in fixed or mobile industrial radiography, the irraditation of food or the processing of products by irradiation, causes it to fail to de-energise at the end of the intended exposure period; or

(b) the malfunction of equipment used in fixed or mobile industrial radiography or gamma irradiation causes a radioactive source to fail to return to its safe position by the normal means at the end of the intended exposure period.

(2) In this paragraph, "radiation generator" has the same meaning as in regulation 2 of the Ionising Radiations Regulations 1985.

Breathing apparatus

9 (1) Any incident in which breathing apparatus malfunctions -

(a) while in use, or

(b) during testing immediately prior to use in such a way that had the malfunction occurred while the apparatus was in use it would have posed a danger to the health or safety of the user.

(2) This paragraph shall not apply to breathing apparatus while it is being -

(a) used in a mine; or

(b) maintained or tested as part of a routine maintenance procedure.

Diving operations

10 Any of the following incidents in relation to a diving operation -

(a) the failure or the endangering of -

(i) any lifting equipment associated with the diving operation, or

(ii) life support equipment, including control panels, hoses and breathing apparatus,

which puts a diver at risk;

(b) any damage to, or endangering of, the dive platform, or any failure of the dive platform to remain on station, which puts a diver at risk;

(c) the trapping of a diver;

(d) any explosion in the vicinity of a diver; or

(e) any uncontrolled ascent or any omitted decompression which puts a diver at risk.

Collapse of scaffolding

11 The complete or partial collapse of -

(a) any scaffold which is -

(i) more than 5 metres in height which results in a substantial part of the scaffold falling or overturning; or

(ii) erected over or adjacent to water in circumstances such that there would be a risk of drowning to a person falling from the scaffold into the water; or

(b) the suspension arrangements (including any outrigger) of any slung or suspended scaffold which causes a working platform or cradle to fall.

Train collisions

12 Any unintended collision of a train with any other train or vehicle, other than one reportable under Part IV of this Schedule, which caused, or might have caused, the death of, or major injury to, any person.

Wells

13 Any of the following incidents in relation to a well (other than a well sunk for the purpose of the abstraction of water) -

(a) a blow-out (that is to say an uncontrolled flow of well-fluids from a well);

(b) the coming into operation of a blow-out prevention or diversion system to control a flow from a well where normal control procedures fail;

(c) the detection of hydrogen sulphide in the course of operations at a well or in samples of well-fluids from a well where the presence of hydrogen sulphide in the reservoir being drawn on by the well was not anticipated by the responsible person before that detection;

(d) the taking of precautionary measures additional to any contained in the original drilling programme following failure to maintain a planned minimum separation distance between wells drilled from a particular installation; or

(e) the mechanical failure of any safety critical element of a well (and for this purpose the safety critical element of a well is any part of a well whose failure would cause or contribute to, or whose purpose is to prevent or limit the effect of, the unintentional release of fluids from a well or a reservoir being drawn on by a well).

Pipelines or pipeline works

14 The following incidents in respect of a pipeline or pipeline works -

(a) the uncontrolled or accidental escape of anything from, or inrush of anything into, a pipeline which has the potential to cause the death of, major injury or damage to the health of any person or which results in the pipeline being shut down for more than 24 hours;

(b) the unintentional ignition of anything in a pipeline or of anything which, immediately before it was ignited, was in a pipeline;

(c) any damage to any part of a pipeline which has the potential to cause the death of, major injury or damage to the health of any person or which results in the pipeline being shut down for more than 24 hours;

(d) any substantial and unintentional change in the position of a pipeline requiring immediate attention to safeguard the integrity or safety of a pipeline;

(e) any unintentional change in the subsoil or seabed in the vicinity of a pipeline which has the potential to affect the integrity or safety of a pipeline;

Schedule 2, Part I

(f) *any failure of any pipeline isolation device, equipment or system which has the potential to cause the death of, major injury or damage to the health of any person or which results in the pipeline being shut down for more than 24 hours; or*

(g) *any failure of equipment involved with pipeline works which has the potential to cause the death of, major injury or damage to the health of any person.*

Fairground equipment

15 *The following incidents on fairground equipment in use or under test -*

(a) *the failure of any load-bearing part;*

(b) *the failure of any part designed to support or restrain passengers; or*

(c) *the derailment or the unintended collision of cars or trains.*

Carriage of dangerous substances by road

16 *(1)* *Any incident involving a road tanker or tank container used for the carriage of a dangerous substance in which -*

(a) *the road tanker or vehicle carrying the tank container overturns (including turning onto its side);*

(b) *the tank carrying the dangerous substance is seriously damaged;*

(c) *there is an uncontrolled release or escape of the dangerous substance being carried; or*

(d) *there is a fire involving the dangerous substance being carried.*

(2) *In this paragraph, "carriage", "dangerous substance", "road tanker" and "tank container" have the same meanings as in regulation 2(1) of the Road Traffic (Carriage of Dangerous Substances in Road Tankers and Tank Containers) Regulations 1992.*

17 *(1)* *Any incident involving a vehicle used for the carriage of a dangerous substance, other than a vehicle to which paragraph 16 applies, where there is -*

(a) *an uncontrolled release or escape of the dangerous substance being carried in such a quantity as to have the potential to cause the death of, or major injury to, any person; or*

(b) *a fire which involves the dangerous substance being carried.*

(2) *In this paragraph, "carriage" and "dangerous substance" have the same meanings as in regulation 2(1) of the Road Traffic (Carriage of Dangerous Substances in Packages etc.) Regulations 1992.*

Dangerous occurrences which are reportable except in relation to offshore workplaces

Collapse of building or structure

18 *Any unintended collapse or partial collapse of -*

Schedule

2, Part I

(a) any building or structure (whether above or below ground) under construction, reconstruction, alteration or demolition which involves a fall of more than 5 tonnes of material;

(b) any floor or wall of any building (whether above or below ground) used as a place of work; or

(c) any false-work.

Explosion or fire

19 An explosion or fire occurring in any plant or premises which results in the stoppage of that plant or as the case may be the suspension of normal work in those premises for more than 24 hours, where the explosion or fire was due to the ignition of any material.

Escape of flammable substances

20 (1) The sudden, uncontrolled release -

(a) inside a building -

(i) of 100 kilograms or more of a flammable liquid,

(ii) of 10 kilograms or more of a flammable liquid at a temperature above its normal boiling point, or

(iii) of 10 kilograms or more of a flammable gas; or

(b) in the open air, of 500 kilograms or more of any of the substances referred to in sub-paragraph (a) above.

(2) In this paragraph, "flammable liquid" and "flammable gas" mean respectively a liquid and a gas so classified in accordance with regulation 5(2), (3) or (5) of the Chemicals (Hazard Information and Packaging for Supply) Regulations 1994.

Escape of substances

21 The accidental release or escape of any substance in a quantity sufficient to cause the death, major injury or any other damage to the health of any person.

Guide

Schedule 2, Part I

101 The list of dangerous occurrences is designed to obtain information primarily about incidents which have a high potential to cause death or serious injury (even though they do not actually cause death or reportable injury), but which happen relatively infrequently. Collecting the information gives the enforcing authorities the opportunity to learn about the circumstances in which they occur and about their causes. This adds to the wider pool of information which can be used to help business in accident prevention work.

102 In some cases it may not be clear immediately whether an incident has a high potential to cause injury. In such cases it is better for the responsible person to make a judgement so a prompt report can be made, rather than waiting until the potential to cause injury is confirmed by tests, further investigation etc. Such a delay could lead to the loss of valuable information relating to the incident.

103 The following explanatory notes on the definitions of the dangerous occurrences in Part I of Schedule 2 (the general list) may be helpful to those

who are uncertain about the reportability of particular incidents (the paragraph numbers are those of the definitions in the Schedule).

104 The term 'plant' is used on a number of occasions in this schedule. This is defined in HSW Act as including any machinery, equipment or appliance.

Lifting machinery (paragraph 1)

105 The definition covers the collapse of any of the machinery or equipment listed, the overturning of any such machinery or equipment or the failure of any loadbearing part of it, whether used for lifting goods, materials or passengers. It does not cover the failure of ancillary equipment such as electric operating buttons or radius indicators.

106 The phrase 'mobile powered access platform' means any platform where the movement of the platform itself is powered, and not necessarily the movement of its supporting vehicle. Power elevated platforms mounted on manually moved vehicles are included. Fixed or mobile tower scaffolds are not included.

107 Incidents involving cranes must be reported irrespective of the nature of the work being done, and reports must not be restricted to those involving lifting and lowering. For example, a collapse or overturning when a machine is being used for drop balling must be included.

108 A 'pile-driving frame or rig' includes a bored piling rig or a percussion piling rig comprising substantially a crane with a jib, normally mounted on crawler tracks, which has been adapted by the addition of pile-driving parts.

Pressure systems (paragraph 2)

109 The definition covers the failure of closed vessels or associated pipework with the potential to cause the death of any person. Vessels and associated pipework subjected to either positive or negative internal pressure are included by this definition.

110 It applies to any such vessel whatever its contents, that is to a vessel containing air, steam, water, or any other gas, vapour or liquid. It applies to moveable as well as to fixed vessels.

111 Incidents requiring notification due to having, 'the potential to cause death of any person', would include: scaldings or burns arising from contact with steam, hot water or other hot liquids, liquors, products or substances; and immersion or splashing with chemicals.

112 Other examples of incidents which might be notifiable as having 'potential to cause death' would be those where a person was either struck by or could potentially have been struck by a projectile emitted from the failure of a closed vessel under pressure. In the event of an explosion, this might be a fixture or component, the vessel itself, or a secondary projectile arising from the destruction of structures close to the vessel: for example, falling debris such as masonry or window glass, or shrapnel from buildings or other structures affected by the release of stored energy arising from the failure of the vessel.

113 However, incidents arising due to the failure of a closed vessel, such as the explosion of an oven in a bakery, due to a build up of fuel gases arising, for example, from a defective flame failure device would be excluded from this category of dangerous occurrence. It would be more appropriate to notify such an incident as an 'Explosion or fire', under Schedule 1: Part I, paragraph 19.

Freight containers (paragraph 3)

114 This definition covers any container which is an article of transport equipment and is:

(a) permanent in character and strong enough for repeated use;

(b) designed to enable the transport of goods by one or more modes of transport without intermediate reloading;

(c) designed to be secured or readily handled or both, having corner fittings for these purposes; and

(d) of a size such that the area enclosed by the outer bottom corners is either:

  (i) if the container is fitted with top corner fittings, at least 7 square metres; or

  (ii) in any other case, at least 14 square metres.

115 The definition covers a container when carried on a chassis but the term 'container' does not include:

(a) a vehicle or packaging;

(b) any article of transport equipment designed solely for use in air transport; or

(c) a swap body (road or rail container without stacking capability and top lift facilities) except when it is carried by or on board a sea-going ship and is not mounted on a road vehicle or rail wagon.

116 The term 'corner fittings' used above means an arrangement of apertures and faces at either the top or the bottom or both at the top and the bottom of the container for the purposes of handling, stacking and securing or any one of those purposes.

Overhead electric lines (paragraph 4)

117 Paragraph 4 refers to incidents involving uninsulated, live, overhead electric lines carrying more than 200 volts. Examples of the kinds of incident which are covered and which must be notified and reported are:

(a) accidental contact of a mobile crane or a vehicle with an overhead line;

(b) accidental contact with an overhead line by something being carried or lifted; and

(c) the collapse of something (eg an engineering structure, a building, a tree during felling operations) across an overhead line.

Electrical short circuit (paragraph 5)

118 Where the failure of an item of electrical equipment results in a fire or explosion, the failure is reportable as a dangerous occurrence if the equipment concerned is rendered unusable for over 24 hours, or if the occurrence was one with the potential to cause the death of any person. The incident is reportable even if the system in which the damaged equipment was installed is put back

Guide

into service using new equipment within 24 hours. In such a case an assessment should be made on how long a repair to the damaged equipment would have taken had it been attempted.

Explosives (paragraph 6)

119 This definition covers incidents arising in a work situation from the use of explosives or from the storage of explosives in premises registered under the Explosives Act 1875. Incidents arising from the storage or use of explosives in factories, magazines or stores licensed under the Explosives Act 1875 are notifiable under that Act and, therefore, not under these Regulations.

Biological agents (paragraph 7)

120 Guidance on the definition of 'biological agents' is given under Schedule 1. Severe human infection can be regarded as that caused by biological agents in Hazard Groups 3 and 4 as defined in COSHH 1994 Schedule 9, paragraph 3(4) and as illustrated in the Approved list of biological agents in the publication *Categorisation of biological agents according to hazard and categories of containment 1995*[7] or otherwise being agents classified provisionally by an employer as being in one of those groups (COSHH Schedule 9, paragraph 3(3)).

Malfunction of radiation generators, etc (paragraph 8)

121 There are two types of equipment whose malfunction is covered here: radiation generators and equipment using radioactive sources (eg gamma ray sources). The Ionising Radiations Regulations 1985 define a radiation generator as any apparatus (except cathode ray tubes and visual display units) in which charged particles are accelerated in a vacuum vessel through a potential difference of more than 5 kV. The types of radiation generator to which the notification requirements apply would include X-ray generators, linear accelerators and electron beam generators as well as other types of particle accelerators.

122 The processes covered include all types of industrial radiography - such as radiography in fixed enclosures, site radiography, and radiography in closed cabinets. Irradiation of food and processing of products by irradiation are high dose treatments and cover panoramic systems as well as self-contained units. In each case it is the failure of the means for de-energising the radiation generator at the end of the intended exposure period that constitutes a notifiable dangerous occurrence.

123 Also notifiable are incidents where equipment malfunction causes a radioactive source to fail to return to a safe (shielded) position at the end of the intended exposure period. The sources will commonly be gamma ray sources, but in industrial radiography could be beta ray or neutron sources. The processes covered once again include all types of industrial radiography, and use of gamma irradiation equipment (panoramic or self-contained). The type of equipment must be such that the source goes from a safe state to an exposed state in use, and operation of manual or automatic control systems normally returns the source to its shielded state. Any malfunction affecting the equipment and its control system causing the failure of the source to return to this state at the end of the intended exposure period constitutes a notifiable dangerous occurrence.

124 These incidents must be notified whether or not any person is exposed to ionising radiation as a result of the incident occurring. The notification of cases

Guide

in which people receive excessive doses of ionising radiation is covered by the Ionising Radiations Regulations 1985 in addition to these requirements.

125 Other types of escape from control of the radioactive source (eg through leakage of the radioactive material out of a sealed source, or loss or theft of equipment containing a source) are also covered by the Ionising Radiations Regulations 1985 and are, therefore, not notifiable under RIDDOR (see regulation 10).

126 It should be noted that malfunctions of X-ray equipment and gamma radiography equipment (including pipeline crawlers), used in the non-destructive testing of pipeline welds, may lead to dangerous occurrences reportable under this heading.

Breathing apparatus (paragraph 9)

127 This definition applies to breathing apparatus used under water as well as in contaminated atmospheres or where there may be a lack of oxygen. It refers to a session of use of the apparatus during or immediately before which a malfunction is detected. The malfunction may be present and be detected immediately before the session (including any testing by the wearer immediately before use), or it may occur at some point after the session has started. If a serious malfunction is not detected in good time and the wearer suffers a major injury, then the incident will be reportable under regulation 3(1).

128 The term 'malfunction' does not include leakage into a face mask due to a poor fit to the face or a failure caused by an external source such as damage due to entanglement or falling debris.

Diving operations (paragraph 10)

129 The phrase 'which puts a diver at risk' would include the potential for a fatality, major injury or reportable disease.

Collapse of scaffolding (paragraph 11)

130 The incidents covered here are those involving any 'scaffold'. This would, for example, include any tower, trestle, slung or suspended scaffold. Incidents involving the failure of the suspension arrangements of slung or suspended scaffolds are also covered if the failure causes a working platform or cradle to fall. Reportable failures of suspension arrangements would include failures of outriggers, roof rigs or suspension ropes or winches.

131 The figure of 5 metres used in relation to the height of scaffolding refers to the height of the scaffolding itself from whatever base and not necessarily to the distance between the top of the scaffold and the ground.

Train collisions (paragraph 12)

132 This dangerous occurrence applies to railways not covered by Part IV of Schedule 2 (those regarded as 'relevant transport systems'). It therefore applies to collisions between rail-mounted locomotives or trains and other vehicles within factory premises or dock premises.

Schedule 2, Part I

Wells (paragraph 13)

133 The incidents listed are reportable in respect of all wells, both onshore and offshore, drilled for the exploration or exploitation of oil or gas, including the production of coal bed methane for commercial purposes. They also apply to wells drilled in connection with the exploitation of oil or gas, for example those used to support reservoir pressure through water or gas injection. The following notes refer to the list of incidents:

(a) Reports are required for all blowouts, including those of limited duration.

(b) Reports are required for all incidents where a blowout preventer is closed or a diverter is operated to control an unplanned flow into the well-bore from the adjoining formations, but not where flow is planned as part of an operation. This includes 'underground blowouts', where the well fluids flow to subsurface rock formations rather than to the surface. Reports are not required where flow is due solely to variations in the density of fluid across pipe installed in the well bore, an effect commonly known as 'U-tubing'; nor where it is known that mud previously lost to the formation is subsequently returned, an effect commonly known as 'ballooning' or 'breathing'.

(c) All unplanned well intersections, where a well is unintentionally drilled into an existing one, are reportable. 'Near misses' should also be reported if normal drilling operations have to be interrupted to take remedial action to reduce the risk of collision.

(d) Failures of the primary pressure containment envelope of a well or of safety devices, namely blowout preventers or surface, subsea and sub-surface safety valves should be reported where there is a major loss of pressure integrity requiring immediate remedial action. It is not necessary to report minor leaks or failures found and rectified during routine maintenance, including replacement of worn components. Significant leakages around a well of hydrocarbon gas from shallow formations should also be reported.

Pipelines or pipeline works (paragraph 14)

134 The incidents listed are reportable in respect of both onshore and offshore pipelines or pipeline works (see paragraph x for definitions of 'pipeline' and 'pipeline works'). The person responsible for reporting incidents (a) to (f) is the owner of the pipeline. Incidents falling under (g) are reportable by the person in charge of the place where the works (such as laying a pipe) are going on, except that if the incident involves a diving operation, the diving contractor will be responsible for reporting. The following notes refer to the list of incidents:

(a) This is not intended to include minor leaks from pipelines eg small leaks from valve stems, flanges etc. However, sudden or uncontrolled escapes requiring immediate attention or action should be reported.

(b) Examples of reportable damage with the potential for harm would include such things as gouging, denting, buckling etc caused by external interference requiring immediate action. Such damage may or may not have resulted in escape of the pipeline contents. Shutdown following discovery of substantial internal or external corrosion such that it would not be safe to continue operating the pipeline should also be reported. External coating damage without damage to the underlying substrate would not be reportable.

Guide

(c) Examples of reportable occurrences would include movement of offshore pipelines following development of critical 'spans' and subsequent instability or displacement due to wave action or boat impact. Occurrences not reportable would include spans detected and rectified as a result of routine inspection activities.

(d) Such occurrences would include landslips, subsidence etc onshore, in the vicinity of pipelines, and similar movement in the seabed.

(e) Isolation devices would include both equipment associated with normal operation of the pipeline such as emergency shut down systems and devices used during non routine activities involving stopples, ice plugs etc.

(f) This is intended to cover such things as failure of tensioners or lay down equipment offshore and winching/tensioning equipment at onshore landfall sites.

Carriage of dangerous substances by road: tankers and tank containers (paragraph 16)

135 Incidents involving road tankers and tank containers to which the Road Traffic (Carriage of Dangerous Substances in Road Tankers and Tank Containers) Regulations 1992 apply, are covered by this definition.

136 Any overturning incident, including a vehicle rolling over on to its side is covered by paragraph 16(1)(a) and must be reported, regardless of whether or not damage is caused to the tank containing the dangerous substance.

137 The term 'seriously damaged' in paragraph 16(1)(b) includes damage which is thought to be likely to require significant repairs to the tank, followed by examination, testing and certification by a competent person (in accordance with regulation 7(1) of the above-mentioned 'Tankers' Regulations), before it can be used again.

138 Paragraph 16(1)(c) covers all uncontrolled releases or escapes of dangerous substances, whether from valves, pipework or the body of the tanker or tank container, except for normal relieving of gas or vapour through pressure relief devices. However, relieving of gas or vapour through a pressure relief system would be covered if this was, for example brought about by an incident such as a fire in which the flames impinged on the tank.

139 Any fire involving the dangerous substance being conveyed must be reported, whether it is due to ignition of the dangerous substance itself, the ignition of fuel used by the vehicle or to ignition by any other source of fire.

Carriage of dangerous substances by road other than by tankers and tank containers (paragraph 17)

140 Paragraph 17 is concerned with incidents involving the carriage by road of the dangerous substances defined by regulation 2(1) of the Road Traffic (Carriage of Dangerous Substances in Packages etc) Regulations 1992.

141 The incidents covered by paragraph 17(1)(a) are uncontrolled releases or escapes of such substances, while being conveyed by road, from packages or containers such as cartons, cans, bottles, carboys, gas cylinders, drums, sacks and small tank containers. They include releases or escapes due to breakage or damage: during loading or unloading; resulting from poor stowage or insecure loads; or resulting from road traffic accidents.

Schedule 2, Part I

Guide

142 Paragraph 17(1)(b) covers any fire involving the dangerous substance while being carried by road in any package or container, or by any other means except the tankers or tank containers covered by paragraph 16, regardless of the source of the fire.

NB the Dangerous Occurrences defined in paragraphs 18 to 21 of Schedule 2 do not apply to offshore workplaces.

Collapse of building or structure (paragraph 18)

143 The 'false-work' referred to in paragraph 8(c) means any temporary structure used to support a permanent structure during its erection and until that structure becomes self-supporting.

144 Examples of incidents reportable under paragraph 8(b) would include:

(a) the collapse of a heavily loaded floor in a building;

(b) the collapse of any floor or wall as a result of a vehicle colliding with a building used as work premises.

Explosion or fire (paragraph 19)

145 This definition covers the more serious fires and explosions which might arise from the ignition of any material on the premises. Examples of the type of incident which would be reportable are:

(a) any fire at a factory or office building, causing the suspension of work activities for more than 24 hours; or

(b) an explosion involving dust in a pneumatic conveying system, causing stoppage of the conveying plant for more than 24 hours.

Escape of flammable substances (paragraph 20)

146 This definition is designed to cover releases of flammable liquids or gasses (eg due to the sudden failure of a storage vessel) where the release, if ignited, would cause a major explosion or fire.

Escape of substances (paragraph 21)

147 The substances covered by this definition may be in any form: liquid, solid (eg powder), gaseous or vapour and may include, for example:

(a) substances which may be hazardous to health (eg asbestos, phosgene, toluene diisocyanate);

(b) substances which may be either corrosive or potentially hazardous by virtue of their temperature or pressure (eg nitric acid, molten metal, liquid nitrogen);

(c) substances which may, depending upon the circumstances of the escape, present a fire or explosion hazard (eg oxygen, acetylene).

Schedule 2, Part I

148 Examples of the kinds of incident involving substances which might be covered by the definition are escapes arising from: the failure or breakage of

Guide

plant, pipes, equipment or apparatus; failures of process control; the operation of a relief valve or bursting disc where the escaping substance is not safely controlled or directed; and spillages from containers and equipment.

149 Releases from plant etc, during the normal course of operation or maintenance (eg during sampling, packaging or draining of lines) that are sufficiently well controlled to ensure that no person is put at risk would not be reportable.

150 The decision as to whether or not an incident is reportable depends upon factors such as: the nature of the substance and its chemical, physical and toxicological properties, the amount which escaped and its dispersal; and whether people could have been present at the time.

Schedule 2, Part I

Regulation 2(1)

Schedule

Part II Dangerous occurrences which are reportable in relation to mines

Fire or ignition of gas

22 The ignition, below ground, of any gas (other than gas in a safety lamp) or of any dust.

23 The accidental ignition of any gas in part of a firedamp drainage system on the surface or in an exhauster house.

24 The outbreak of any fire below ground.

25 An incident where any person in consequence of any smoke or any other indication that a fire may have broken out below ground has been caused to leave any place pursuant to either Regulation 11(1) of the Coal and Other Mines (Fire and Rescue) Regulations 1956 or section 79 of the Mines and Quarries Act 1954.

26 The outbreak of any fire on the surface which endangers the operation of any winding or haulage apparatus installed at a shaft or unwalkable outlet or of any mechanically operated apparatus for producing ventilation below ground.

Escape of gas

27 Any violent outburst of gas together with coal or other solid matter into the mine workings except when such outburst is caused intentionally.

Failure of plant or equipment

28 The breakage of any rope, chain, coupling, balance rope, guide rope, suspension gear or other gear used for or in connection with the carrying of persons through any shaft or staple shaft.

29 The breakage or unintentional uncoupling of any rope, chain, coupling, rope tensioning system or other gear used for or in connection with the transport of persons below ground, or breakage of any belt, rope or other gear used for or in connection with a belt conveyor designated by the mine manager as a man-riding conveyor.

30 An incident where any conveyance being used for the carriage of persons is overwound; or any conveyance not being so used is overwound and becomes detached from its winding rope; or any conveyance operated by means of the friction of a rope on a winding sheave is brought to rest by the apparatus provided in the headframe of

2, Part II

the shaft or in the part of the shaft below the lowest landing for the time being in use, being apparatus provided for bringing the conveyance to rest in the event of its being overwound.

31 The stoppage of any ventilating apparatus (other than an auxiliary fan) which causes a substantial reduction in ventilation of the mine lasting for a period exceeding 30 minutes, except when for the purpose of planned maintenance.

32 The collapse of any headframe, winding engine house, fan house or storage bunker.

Breathing apparatus

33 At any mine an incident where -

(a) breathing apparatus or a smoke helmet or other apparatus serving the same purpose or a self-rescuer, while being used, fails to function safely or develops a defect likely to affect its safe working; or

(b) immediately after using and arising out of the use of breathing apparatus or a smoke helmet or other apparatus serving the same purpose or a self-rescuer, any person receives first-aid or medical treatment by reason of his unfitness or suspected unfitness at the mine.

Injury by explosion of blasting material etc

34 An incident in which any person suffers an injury (not being a major injury or one reportable under regulation 3(2)) which results from an explosion or discharge of any blasting material or device within the meaning of section 69(4) of the Mines and Quarries Act 1954 for which he receives first-aid or medical treatment at the mine.

Use of emergency escape apparatus

35 An incident where any apparatus is used (other than for the purpose of training and practice) which has been provided at the mine in accordance with regulation 4 of the Mines (Safety of Exit) Regulations 1988 or where persons leave the mine when apparatus and equipment normally used by persons to leave the mine is unavailable.

Inrush of gas or water

36 Any inrush of noxious or flammable gas from old workings.

37 Any inrush of water or material which flows when wet from any source.

Insecure tip

38 Any movement of material or any fire or any other event which indicates that a tip to which Part I of the Mines and Quarries (Tips) Act 1969 applies, is or is likely to become insecure.

Locomotives

39 Any incident where an underground locomotive when not used for testing purposes is brought to rest by means other than its safety circuit protective devices or normal service brakes.

Schedule 2, Part II

Falls of ground

40 Any fall of ground, not being part of the normal operations at a mine, which results from a failure of an underground support system and prevents persons travelling through the area affected by the fall or which otherwise exposes them to danger.

Schedule 2, Part III

Part III Dangerous occurrences which are reportable in relation to quarries

Collapse of storage bunkers

41 The collapse of any storage bunker.

Sinking of craft

42 The sinking of any water-borne craft or hovercraft.

Injuries

43 (1) An incident in which any person suffers an injury (not otherwise reportable under these Regulations) which results from an explosion or from the discharge of any explosives for which he receives first-aid or medical treatment at the quarry.

(2) In this paragraph, "explosives" has the same meaning as in regulation 2(1) of the Quarries (Explosives) Regulations 1988.

Projection of substances outside quarry

44 Any incident in which any substance is ascertained to have been projected beyond a quarry boundary as a result of blasting operations in circumstances in which any person was or might have been endangered.

Misfires

45 Any misfire, as defined by regulation 2(1) of the Quarries (Explosives) Regulations 1988.

Insecure tips

46 Any event (including any movement of material or any fire) which indicates that a tip, to which Part I of the Mines and Quarries (Tips) Act 1969 applies, is or is likely to become insecure.

Movement of slopes or faces

47 Any movement or failure of an excavated slope or face which -

(a) has the potential to cause the death of any person; or

(b) adversely affects any building, contiguous land, transport system, footpath, public utility or service, watercourse, reservoir or area of public access.

Explosions or fires in vehicles or plant

48 (1) Any explosion or fire occurring in any large vehicle or mobile plant which results in the stoppage of that vehicle or plant for more than 24 hours and which affects -

Schedule

2, Part III

(a) *any place where persons normally work; or*

(b) *the route of egress from such a place.*

(2) *In this paragraph, "large vehicle or mobile plant" means -*

(a) *a dump truck having a load capacity of at least 50 tonnes; or*

(b) *an excavator having a bucket capacity of at least 5 cubic metres.*

Schedule

2, Part IV

Part IV Dangerous occurrences which are reportable in respect of relevant transport systems

Accidents to passenger trains

49 *Any collision in which a passenger train collides with another train.*

50 *Any case where a passenger train or any part of such a train unintentionally leaves the rails.*

Accidents not involving passenger trains

51 *Any collision between trains, other than one between a passenger train and another train, on a running line where any train sustains damage as a result of the collision, and any such collision in a siding which results in a running line being obstructed.*

52 *Any derailment, of a train other than a passenger train, on a running line, except a derailment which occurs during shunting operations and does not obstruct any other running line.*

53 *Any derailment, of a train other than a passenger train, in a siding which results in a running line being obstructed.*

Accidents involving any kind of train

54 *Any case of a train striking a buffer stop, other than in a siding, where damage is caused to the train.*

55 *Any case of a train striking any cattle or horse, whether or not damage is caused to the train, or striking any other animal if, in consequence, damage (including damage to the windows of the driver's cab but excluding other damage consisting solely in the breakage of glass) is caused to the train necessitating immediate temporary or permanent repair.*

56 *Any case of a train on a running line striking or being struck by any object which causes damage (including damage to the windows of the driver's cab but excluding other damage consisting solely in the breakage of glass) necessitating immediate temporary or permanent repair or which might have been liable to derail the train.*

57 *Any case of a train, other than one on a railway, striking or being struck by a road vehicle.*

58 *Any case of a passenger train, or any other train not fitted with continuous self-applying brakes, becoming unintentionally divided.*

59 (1) Any of the following classes of accident which occurs or is discovered whilst the train is on a running line -

(a) the failure of an axle;

(b) the failure of a wheel or tyre, including a tyre loose on its wheel;

(c) the failure of a rope or the fastenings thereof or of the winding plant or equipment involved in working an incline;

(d) any fire, severe electrical arcing or fusing in or on any part of a passenger train or a train carrying dangerous goods;

(e) in the case of any train other than a passenger train, any severe electrical arcing or fusing, or any fire which was extinguished by a fire-fighting service;or

(f) any other failure of any part of a train which is likely to cause an accident to that or any other train or to kill or injure any person.

(2) In this paragraph "dangerous goods" has the same meaning as in regulation 1(2) of the Carriage of Dangerous Goods by Rail Regulations 1994.

Accidents and incidents at level crossings

60 Any case of a train striking a road vehicle or gate at a level crossing.

61 Any case of a train running onto a level crossing when not authorised to do so.

62 A failure of the equipment at a level crossing which could endanger users of the road or path crossing the railway.

Accidents involving the permanent way and other works on or connected with a relevant transport system

63 The failure of a rail in a running line or of a rack rail, which results in -

(a) a complete fracture of the rail through its cross-section;or

(b) in a piece becoming detached from the rail which necessitates an immediate stoppage of traffic or the immediate imposition of a speed restriction lower than that currently in force.

64 A buckle of a running line which necessitates an immediate stoppage of traffic or the immediate imposition of a speed restriction lower than that currently in force.

65 Any case of an aircraft or a vehicle of any kind landing on, running onto or coming to rest foul of the line, or damaging the line, which causes damage which obstructs the line or which damages any railway equipment at a level crossing.

66 The runaway of an escalator, lift or passenger conveyor.

67 Any fire or severe arcing or fusing which seriously affects the functioning of signalling equipment.

68 Any fire affecting the permanent way or works of a relevant transport system which necessitates the suspension of services over any line, or the closure of any part of a station or signal box or other premises, for a period -

(a) in the case of a fire affecting any part of a relevant transport system below ground, of more than 30 minutes, and

(b) in any other case, of more than 1 hour.

69 Any other fire which causes damage which has the potential to affect the running of a relevant transport system.

Accidents involving failure of the works on or connected with a relevant transport system

70 (1) The following classes of accident where they are likely either to cause an accident to a train or to endanger any person -

(a) the failure of a tunnel, bridge, viaduct, culvert, station, or other structure or any part thereof including the fixed electrical equipment of an electrified relevant transport system;

(b) any failure in the signalling system which endangers or which has the potential to endanger the safe passage of trains other than a failure of a traffic light controlling the movement of vehicles on a road;

(c) a slip of a cutting or of an embankment;

(d) flooding of the permanent way;

(e) the striking of a bridge by a vessel or by a road vehicle or its load; or

(f) the failure of any other portion of the permanent way or works not specified above.

Incidents of serious congestion

71 Any case where planned procedures or arrangements have been activated in order to control risks arising from an incident of undue passenger congestion at a station unless that congestion has been relieved within a period of time allowed for by those procedures or arrangements.

Incidents of signals passed without authority

72 (1) Any case where a train, travelling on a running line or entering a running line from a siding, passes without authority a signal displaying a stop aspect unless -

(a) the stop aspect was not displayed in sufficient time for the driver to stop safely at the signal; or

(b) the line is equipped with automatic train protection equipment which is in operation.

(2) In this paragraph "automatic train protection equipment" means equipment which automatically controls the speed of a train, either by bringing it to a halt or reducing its speed, in the event that the train passes a signal without authority or exceeds a prescribed speed limit.

Part V Dangerous occurrences which are reportable in respect of an offshore workplace

Release of petroleum hydrocarbon

73 Any unintentional release of petroleum hydrocarbon on or from an offshore installation which -

(a) results in -

(i) a fire or explosion; or

(ii) the taking of action to prevent or limit the consequences of a potential fire or explosion; or

(b) has the potential to cause death or major injury to any person.

Fire or explosion

74 Any fire or explosion at an offshore installation, other than one to which paragraph 73 above applies, which results in the stoppage of plant or the suspension of normal work.

Release or escape of dangerous substances

75 The uncontrolled or unintentional release or escape of any substance (other than petroleum hydrocarbon) on or from an offshore installation which has the potential to cause the death of, major injury to or damage to the health of any person.

Collapses

76 Any unintended collapse of any offshore installation or any unintended collapse of any part thereof or any plant thereon which jeopardises the overall structural integrity of the installation.

Dangerous occurrences

77 Any of the following occurrences having the potential to cause death or major injury -

(a) the failure of equipment required to maintain a floating offshore installation on station;

(b) the dropping of any object on an offshore installation or on an attendant vessel or into the water adjacent to an installation or vessel; or

(c) damage to or on an offshore installation caused by adverse weather conditions.

Collisions

78 Any collision between a vessel or aircraft and an offshore installation which results in damage to the installation, the vessel or the aircraft.

79 Any occurrence with the potential for a collision between a vessel and an offshore installation where, had a collision occurred, it would have been liable to jeopardise the overall structural integrity of the offshore installation.

Schedule 2, Part V

Subsidence or collapse of seabed

80 Any subsidence or local collapse of the seabed likely to affect the foundations of an offshore installation or the overall structural integrity of an offshore installation.

Loss of stability or buoyancy

81 Any incident involving loss of stability or buoyancy of a floating offshore installation.

Evacuation

82 Any evacuation (other than one arising out of an incident reportable under any other provision of these Regulations) of an offshore installation, in whole or part, in the interests of safety.

Falls into water

83 Any case of a person falling more than 2 metres into water (unless the fall results in death or injury required to be reported under sub-paragraphs (a) - (d) of regulation 3 (1)).

Guide Schedule 2, Part V

151 The dangerous occurrences in this part are reportable only if they occur at an offshore workplace (see paragraph 20), ie at or in connection with an offshore installation, offshore well or offshore pipeline. Most of the incidents are further restricted to those involving offshore installations only (see paragraph 19). Note that in this section 'offshore installation' includes subsea units, but excludes tied back wells, pipelines and associated apparatus or works within 500 m of the installation's main structure, and fixed towers not associated with oil and gas activities.

152 Paragraphs 77(g) and 78 extend to activities in connection with offshore installations. Paragraph 83 applies to the full range of 'offshore workplaces' (see paragraph 20).

Release of petroleum hydrocarbon (paragraph 73)

153 This refers to *confirmed* unintentional releases of petroleum hydrocarbons. Suspected releases which turn out to be false (eg spurious alarms) are not reportable.

154 To be reportable, releases must also lead to one of the following outcomes:

(a) (i) *a fire or explosion.* This includes all types of fires, ie flash, jet or pool, regardless of the length of time of burning;

(ii) *action to prevent or limit the consequences of a potential fire or explosion.* A release with the *potential* for fire or explosion would involve a risk of fire or explosion sufficient to require preventive or evasive action. Small gas leaks detected during routine monitoring and maintenance, eg Draeger tube checking on valves, seals, etc where there is limited risk to personnel, need not be reported. To be reportable, the *action* taken must be intended to prevent or limit the consequences of a potential fire or explosion. Simply taking action to confirm a release following an alarm, for example by instrument reading, but which requires no further action, would not be reportable. However, it may precede more direct action which is reportable.

Guide

Examples of actions which would mean that the release is reportable are:

- emergency stoppage of individual plant, either automatically or by operator intervention, to control leakage of process or non-process hydrocarbons;
- stoppage of or suspension of work on a particular process or stoppage of a permit-to-work following confirmation of a hydrocarbon release with a potential for fire or explosion;
- operation of deluge, fixed fire-fighting system, blowdown etc or other preventive or limiting measures as a result of a confirmed hydrocarbon release;
- general shutdown, muster, evacuation of the area, or any combination of these actions following a confirmed release.

(b) *the potential to cause death or major injury to any person.* Hydrocarbon releases not covered by (a)(i) or (a)(ii) above, but which may also give cause for concern (eg where associated with high H_2S toxicity; or where the release is dispersed or exhausts a limited inventory before action can be taken) are also reportable.

Fire or explosion (paragraph 74)

155 This covers fires or explosions not covered by paragraph 73, such as:

- hydrocarbon releases from flares, vents or diverters which exceed operational limits;
- inadvertent internal combustion, for example of unspent fuels within turbines or of flame/explosion propagation within flare systems;
- fires or explosions involving wood, paints, explosives (if not covered by paragraph 6) etc.

Release or escape of dangerous substances (paragraph 75)

156 This covers releases of substances such as stored chemicals, superheated steam, or H_2S where not associated with hydrocarbons.

Collisions (paragraph 79)

157 It will not always be possible to estimate with any accuracy whether a collision could have occurred or what the consequences might have been. HSE is primarily interested to know of incidents in which the duty holder considers there was a significant risk to the installation.

Evacuation (paragraph 82)

158 Full or partial evacuation may be a response to an incident separately reportable under these Regulations (eg a fire or explosion), in which case it is not reportable under this paragraph. Paragraph 82 seeks to identify incidents not otherwise reportable, in which the risks are sufficient to warrant evacuation. It does not cover exercises or precautionary measures.

Schedule 2, Part V

Schedule 3

Reportable diseases

Regulation 5

Schedule

Part I Occupational diseases

(Guidance is given at Paragraph 159 on those items marked with an asterisk)

	Column 1 *Diseases*	*Column 2* *Activities*
	Conditions due to physical agents and the physical demands of work	
1*	*Inflammation, ulceration or malignant disease of the skin due to ionising radiation.*	*Work with ionising radiation.*
2*	*Malignant disease of the bones due to ionising radiation.*	*Work with ionising radiation.*
3*	*Blood dyscrasia due to ionising radiation.*	*Work with ionising radiation.*
4*	*Cataract due to electromagnetic radiation.*	*Work involving exposure to electromagnetic radiation (including radiant heat).*
5*	*Decompression illness.*	*Work involving breathing gases at increased pressure (including diving).*
6	*Barotrauma resulting in lung or other organ damage.*	*Work involving breathing gases at increased pressure (including diving).*
7	*Dysbaric osteonecrosis.*	*Work involving breathing gases at increased pressure (including diving).*
8*	*Cramp of the hand or forearm due to repetitive movements.*	*Work involving prolonged periods of handwriting, typing or other repetitive movements of the fingers, hand or arm.*
9	*Subcutaneous cellulitis of the hand (beat hand).*	*Physically demanding work causing severe or prolonged friction or pressure on the hand.*
10	*Bursitis or subcutaneous cellulitis arising at or about the knee due to severe or prolonged external friction or pressure at or about the knee (beat knee).*	*Physically demanding work causing severe or prolonged friction or pressure at or about the knee.*
11	*Bursitis or subcutaneous cellulitis arising at or about the elbow due to severe or prolonged external friction or pressure at or about the elbow (beat elbow).*	*Physically demanding work causing severe or prolonged friction or pressure at or about the elbow.*
12	*Traumatic inflammation of the tendons of the hand or forearm or of the associated tendon sheaths.*	*Physically demanding work, frequent or repeated movements, constrained postures or extremes of extension or flexion of the hand or wrist.*

3, Part I

Column 1 *Diseases*	*Column 2* *Activities*
13 *Carpal tunnel syndrome.*	*Work involving the use of hand-held vibrating tools.*
*14** *Hand-arm vibration syndrome.*	*Work involving:* *(a)* *the use of chain saws, brush cutters or hand-held or hand-fed circular saws in forestry or woodworking;* *(b)* *the use of hand-held rotary tools in grinding material or in sanding or polishing metal;* *(c)* *the holding of material being ground or metal being sanded or polished by rotary tools;* *(d)* *the use of hand-held percussive metal-working tools or the holding of metal being worked upon by percussive tools in connection with riveting, caulking, chipping, hammering, fettling or swaging;* *(e)* *the use of hand-held powered percussive drills or hand-held powered percussive hammers in mining, quarrying or demolition, or on roads or footpaths (including road construction); or* *(f)* *the holding of material being worked upon by pounding machines in shoe manufacture.*

Infections due to biological agents

15 *Anthrax.*	*(a)* *Work involving handling infected animals, their products or packaging containing infected material; or* *(b)* *work on infected sites.*
16 *Brucellosis.*	*Work involving contact with:* *(a)* *animals or their carcasses (including any parts thereof) infected by brucella or the untreated products of same; or* *(b)* *laboratory specimens or vaccines of or containing brucella.*
17 *(a)* *Avian chlamydiosis.*	*Work involving contact with birds infected with chlamydia psittaci, or the remains or untreated products of such birds.*

Column 1 *Diseases*		*Column 2* *Activities*
	(b) Ovine chlamydiosis.	*Work involving contact with sheep infected with chlamydia psittaci or the remains or untreated products of such sheep.*
*18**	*Hepatitis.*	*Work involving contact with:* *(a) human blood or human blood products; or* *(b) any source of viral hepatitis.*
19	*Legionellosis.*	*Work on or near cooling systems which are located in the workplace and use water; or work on hot water service systems located in the workplace which are likely to be a source of contamination.*
20	*Leptospirosis.*	*(a) Work in places which are or are liable to be infested by rats, fieldmice, voles or other small mammals;* *(b) work at dog kennels or involving the care or handling of dogs; or* *(c) work involving contact with bovine animals or their meat products or pigs or their meat products.*
21	*Lyme disease.*	*Work involving exposure to ticks (including in particular work by forestry workers, rangers, dairy farmers, game keepers and other persons engaged in countryside management).*
22	*Q fever.*	*Work involving contact with animals, their remains or their untreated products.*
23	*Rabies.*	*Work involving handling or contact with infected animals.*
24	*Streptococcus suis.*	*Work involving contact with pigs infected with streptococcus suis, or with the carcasses, products or residues of pigs so affected.*
25	*Tetanus.*	*Work involving contact with soil likely to be contaminated by animals.*
26	*Tuberculosis.*	*Work with persons, animals, human or animal remains or any other material which might be a source of infection.*

Column 1 *Diseases*	Column 2 *Activities*
27 Any infection reliably attributable to the performance of the work specified in the entry opposite hereto.*	*Work with micro-organisms; work with live or dead human beings in the course of providing any treatment or service or in conducting any investigation involving exposure to blood or body fluids; work with animals or any potentially infected material derived from any of the above.*

Conditions due to substances

28 *Poisonings by any of the following:* (a) *acrylamide monomer;* (b) *arsenic or one of its compounds;* (c) *benzene or a homologue of benzene;* (d) *beryllium or one of its compounds;* (e) *cadmium or one of its compounds;* (f) *carbon disulphide;* (g) *diethylene dioxide (dioxan);* (h) *ethylene oxide;* (i) *lead or one of its compounds;* (j) *manganese or one of its compounds;* (k) *mercury or one of its compounds;* (l) *methyl bromide;* (m) *nitrochlorobenzene, or a nitro- or amino- or chloro-derivative of benzene or of a homologue of benzene;* (n) *oxides of nitrogen;* (o) *phosphorus or one of its compounds.*	*Any activity.*
29 *Cancer of a bronchus or lung.*	(a) *Work in or about a building where nickel is produced by decomposition of a gaseous nickel compound or where any industrial process which is ancillary or incidental to that process is carried on; or*

Column 1 *Diseases*		*Column 2* *Activities*
		(b) *work involving exposure to bis(chloromethyl) ether or any electrolytic chromium processes (excluding passivation) which involve hexavalent chromium compounds, chromate production or zinc chromate pigment manufacture.*
30	*Primary carcinoma of the lung where there is accompanying evidence of silicosis.*	*Any occupation in:* *(a)* *glass manufacture;* *(b)* *sandstone tunnelling or quarrying;* *(c)* *the pottery industry;* *(d)* *metal ore mining;* *(e)* *slate quarrying or slate production;* *(f)* *clay mining;* *(g)* *the use of siliceous materials as abrasives;* *(h)* *foundry work;* *(i)* *granite tunnelling or quarrying; or* *(j)* *stone cutting or masonry.*
31	*Cancer of the urinary tract.*	*1* *Work involving exposure to any of the following substances:* *(a)* *beta-naphthylamine or methylene-bis-orthochloroaniline;* *(b)* *diphenyl substituted by at least one nitro or primary amino group or by at least one nitro and primary amino group (including benzidine);* *(c)* *any of the substances mentioned in sub-paragraph (b) above if further ring substituted by halogeno, methyl or methoxy groups, but not by other groups; or* *(d)* *the salts of any of the substances mentioned in sub-paragraphs (a) to (c) above.*

Column 1 Diseases	Column 2 Activities
	2 The manufacture of auramine or magenta.
32 Bladder cancer.	Work involving exposure to aluminium smelting using the Soderberg process.
33 Angiosarcoma of the liver.	(a) Work in or about machinery or apparatus used for the polymerisation of vinyl chloride monomer, a process which, for the purposes of this sub-paragraph, comprises all operations up to and including the drying of the slurry produced by the polymerisation and the packaging of the dried product; or (b) work in a building or structure in which any part of the process referred to in the foregoing sub-paragraph takes place.
34 Peripheral neuropathy.	Work involving the use or handling of or exposure to the fumes of or vapour containing n-hexane or methyl n-butyl ketone.
35 Chrome ulceration of: (a) the nose or throat; or (b) the skin of the hands or forearm.	Work involving exposure to chromic acid or to any other chromium compound.
36 Folliculitis. 37 Acne. 38 Skin cancer.	Work involving exposure to mineral oil, tar, pitch or arsenic.
39 Pneumoconiosis (excluding asbestosis).	1 (a) The mining, quarrying or working of silica rock or the working of dried quartzose sand, any dry deposit or residue of silica or any dry admixture containing such materials (including any activity in which any of the aforesaid operations are carried out incidentally to the mining or quarrying of other minerals or to the manufacture of articles containing crushed or ground silica rock); or

Column 1 *Diseases*	*Column 2* *Activities*
	(b) *the handling of any of the materials specified in the foregoing sub-paragraph in or incidentally to any of the operations mentioned therein or substantial exposure to the dust arising from such operations.*
	2 *The breaking, crushing or grinding of flint, the working or handling of broken, crushed or ground flint or materials containing such flint or substantial exposure to the dust arising from any of such operations.*
	3 *Sand blasting by means of compressed air with the use of quartzose sand or crushed silica rock or flint or substantial exposure to the dust arising from such sand blasting.*
	4 *Work in a foundry or the performance of, or substantial exposure to the dust arising from, any of the following operations:*
	(a) *the freeing of steel castings from adherent siliceous substance; or*
	(b) *the freeing of metal castings from adherent siliceous substance:*
	(i) *by blasting with an abrasive propelled by compressed air, steam or a wheel, or*
	(ii) *by the use of power-driven tools.*
	5 *The manufacture of china or earthenware (including sanitary earthenware, electrical earthenware and earthenware tiles) and any activity involving substantial exposure to the dust arising therefrom.*
	6 *The grinding of mineral graphite or substantial exposure to the dust arising from such grinding.*
	7 *The dressing of granite or any igneous rock by masons, the crushing of such materials or substantial exposure to the dust arising from such operations.*

Column 1 *Diseases*	*Column 2* *Activities*
	8 The use or preparation for use of an abrasive wheel or substantial exposure to the dust arising therefrom.
	9 (a) Work underground in any mine in which one of the objects of the mining operations is the getting of any material;
	(b) the working or handling above ground at any coal or tin mine of any materials extracted therefrom or any operation incidental thereto;
	(c) the trimming of coal in any ship, barge, lighter, dock or harbour or at any wharf or quay; or
	(d) the sawing, splitting or dressing of slate or any operation incidental thereto.
	10 The manufacture or work incidental to the manufacture of carbon electrodes by an industrial undertaking for use in the electrolytic extraction of aluminium from aluminium oxide and any activity involving substantial exposure to the dust therefrom.
	11 Boiler scaling or substantial exposure to the dust arising therefrom.
40 Byssinosis.	*The spinning or manipulation of raw or waste cotton or flax or the weaving of cotton or flax, carried out in each case in a room in a factory, together with any other work carried out in such a room.*
41 Mesothelioma *42 Lung cancer.* *43 Asbestosis.*	*(a) The working or handling of asbestos or any admixture of asbestos;*
	(b) the manufacture or repair of asbestos textiles or other articles containing or composed of asbestos;
	(c) the cleaning of any machinery or plant used in any of the foregoing operations and of any chambers, fixtures and appliances for the collection of asbestos dust; or
	(d) substantial exposure to the dust arising from any of the foregoing operations.

Column 1 *Diseases*	*Column 2* *Activities*
44 *Cancer of the nasal cavity or associated air sinuses.*	1 (a) *Work in or about a building where wooden furniture is manufactured;*
	(b) *work in a building used for the manufacture of footwear or components of footwear made wholly or partly of leather or fibre board; or*
	(c) *work at a place used wholly or mainly for the repair of footwear made wholly or partly of leather or fibre board.*
	2 *Work in or about a factory building where nickel is produced by decomposition of a gaseous nickel compound or in any process which is ancillary or incidental thereto.*
45* *Occupational dermatitis.*	*Work involving exposure to any of the following agents:*
	(a) *epoxy resin systems;*
	(b) *formaldehyde and its resins;*
	(c) *metalworking fluids;*
	(d) *chromate (hexavalent and derived from trivalent chromium);*
	(e) *cement, plaster or concrete;*
	(f) *acrylates and methacrylates;*
	(g) *colophony (rosin) and its modified products;*
	(h) *glutaraldehyde;*
	(i) *mercaptobenzothiazole, thiurams, substituted paraphenylene-diamines and related rubber processing chemicals;*
	(j) *biocides, anti-bacterials, preservatives or disinfectants;*
	(k) *organic solvents;*
	(l) *antibiotics and other pharmaceuticals and therapeutic agents;*

Column 1 Diseases	Column 2 Activities
	(m) *strong acids, strong alkalis, strong solutions (eg brine) and oxidising agents including domestic bleach or reducing agents;*
	(n) *hairdressing products including in particular dyes, shampoos, bleaches and permanent waving solutions;*
	(o) *soaps and detergents;*
	(p) *plants and plant-derived material including in particular especially the daffodil, tulip and chrysanthemum families, the parsley family (carrots, parsnips, parsley and celery), garlic and onion, hardwoods and the pine family;*
	(q) *fish, shell-fish or meat;*
	(r) *sugar or flour; or*
	(s) *any other known irritant or sensitising agent including in particular any chemical bearing the warning "may cause sensitisation by skin contact" or "irritating to the skin".*
46 *Extrinsic alveolitis (including farmer's lung).*	*Exposure to moulds, fungal spores or heterologous proteins during work in:*
	(a) *agriculture, horticulture, forestry, cultivation of edible fungi or malt-working;*
	(b) *loading, unloading or handling mouldy vegetable matter or edible fungi whilst same is being stored;*
	(c) *caring for or handling birds; or*
	(d) *handling bagasse.*
*47** *Occupational asthma.*	*Work involving exposure to any of the following agents:*
	(a) *isocyanates;*
	(b) *platinum salts;*

Column 1 Diseases	Column 2 Activities
	(c) fumes or dust arising from the manufacture, transport or use of hardening agents (including epoxy resin curing agents) based on phthalic anhydride, tetrachlorophthalic anhydride, trimellitic anhydride or triethylene-tetramine;
	(d) fumes arising from the use of rosin as a soldering flux;
	(e) proteolytic enzymes;
	(f) animals including insects and other arthropods used for the purposes of research or education or in laboratories;
	(g) dusts arising from the sowing, cultivation, harvesting, drying, handling, milling, transport or storage of barley, oats, rye, wheat or maize or the handling, milling, transport or storage of meal or flour made therefrom;
	(h) antibiotics;
	(i) cimetidine;
	(j) wood dust;
	(k) ispaghula;
	(l) castor bean dust;
	(m) ipecacuanha;
	(n) azodicarbonamide;
	(o) animals including insects and other arthropods (whether in their larval forms or not) used for the purposes of pest control or fruit cultivation or the larval forms of animals used for the purposes of research or education or in laboratories;
	(p) glutaraldehyde;
	(q) persulphate salts or henna;
	(r) crustaceans or fish or products arising from these in the food processing industry;
	(s) reactive dyes;

Schedule 3, Part I

Column 1 *Diseases*	*Column 2* *Activities*
	(t) *soya bean;*
	(u) *tea dust;*
	(v) *green coffee bean dust;*
	(w) *fumes from stainless steel welding;*
	(x) *any other sensitising agent, including in particular any chemical bearing the warning "may cause sensitisation by inhalation".*

Guide

Schedule 3, Part I

Guidance on diseases/conditions in Schedule 3, Part I

159 The following table gives notes on those diseases in Schedule 3, Part 1 which have been highlighted with an asterisk.

Disease/condition	*Schedule 3, Part 1, Item No*	*Guidance*
Inflammation, ulceration or malignant disease of the skin due to ionising radiation	1	The following conditions should always be reported under this heading: ● erythema, primary or secondary radiation burns; ● subsequent acute or chronic ulcers. Non melanoma skin cancer is common in the general population. It need only be reported if the history of exposure or the features of the condition suggest an association with ionising radiation. This would be the case in respect of: ● squamous cell carcinoma occurring after high-dose exposure or at the site of past ulceration; ● basal cell carcinoma where features such as multiple lesions suggest a possible relationship with ionising radiation.
Malignant disease of the bones due to ionising radiation	2	Sarcoma of the bone is reportable. Secondary malignant disease of the bone is not reportable.

Disease/condition	*Schedule 3, Part 1, Item No*	*Guidance*
Blood dyscrasia due to ionising radiation	3	The following conditions are reportable: ● acute changes in the blood picture, eg reduction in the number of small lymphocytes where no other clinical causes are established and there is reason to believe that this is the result of acute exposure to ionising radiation; ● acute leukaemias; ● chronic myeloid leukaemia; ● Non-Hodgkins lymphoma; ● aplastic anaemia. Polycythaemia rubra vera is not reportable.
Cataract due to electromagnetic radiation	4	Cataracts are common in the general population. They need not be reported where there is good reason to believe that they were not caused at work by exposure to electromagnetic radiation (eg ionising radiation, microwaves). Cataracts resulting from exposure to ionising radiations or to radiant heat typically occur at the posterior pole of the lens. Intense exposure to microwave radiation may result in anterior or posterior subcapsular opacities.
Decompression illness	5	Decompression illness is defined as any signs or symptoms arising from the presence of gas within tissues or vessels of the body following a reduction in ambient pressure.
Cramp of the hand or forearm due to repetitive movements	8	Cramp is reportable where it is a chronic condition linked to repetitive work movements. The condition is usually characterised by the inability to carry out a sequence of what were previously well co-ordinated movements. An acute incident of cramp which may occur in the course of work is not reportable.
Hand-arm vibration syndrome (HAVS)	14	Workers whose hands are regularly exposed to high vibration, for example in industries where vibratory tools and machines are used, may suffer from several kinds of injury to the hands and

Disease/condition	Schedule 3, Part 1, Item No	Guidance
		arm including impaired blood circulation and damage to the nerves and muscles. The injuries collectively are known as 'hand-arm vibration syndrome'. Other names used in industry include - vibration white finger, dead finger, dead hand and white finger. The severity of the vascular and neurological effects is indicated using an agreed classification system, the Stockholm Workshop Scales. More information on this and HAVS is contained in HSE guidance *Hand-arm vibration*[8].
Hepatitis	18	The likely sources of hepatitis are: Hepatitis A and E - human excreta and objects and consumables contaminated principally by excreta from people infected with hepatitis A or E virus. Hepatitis B,C and D - human blood and body fluids from people infected with hepatitis viruses B,C and D*, objects contaminated by blood and body fluids, particularly sharp objects such as used hypodermic needles, contaminated broken glassware and other items where these penetrate the skin or otherwise may act as a vehicle for transmission of infection. Other, as yet uncharacterised, forms of viral hepatitis are known to exist. * *hepatitis D virus is only infectious in the presence of concomitant or pre-existing infection with hepatitis B.*
Any infection reliably attributable to the performance of the work specified opposite hereto	27	Many minor infections such as those causing bouts of diarrhoea and respiratory complaints such as colds and bronchitis are common in the community and everyone is exposed to them. These minor illnesses cannot generally be attributed to infection contracted at work and they are generally not reportable. However, where there is reasonable circumstantial evidence, for example, known contact with the infectious agent in laboratory work, a report should be made.

Guide

Schedule 3, Part I

Disease/condition	*Schedule 3, Part 1, Item No*	*Guidance*
Occupational dermatitis	45	*Item 45 (s) - any other known irritant or sensitising agent.* A list of examples of 'other known irritants or sensitising agents' is given in Appendix 1 of HSE Guidance Note MS 24, *Health Surveillance of Occupational Skin Disease*[9], and further guidance is available in the references provided in Appendix 3 of the document. Dermatitis can be caused by exposure to a range of common agents found outside the workplace. If there is good evidence that the condition has been caused solely by such exposure rather than by exposure to an agent at work it need not be reported.
Occupational asthma	47	*Item 47(x) - any other sensitising agent.* For examples of agents reported to have caused occupational asthma see *Preventing Asthma at Work - How to Control Respiratory Sensitisers*[10]. Asthma is a common condition in the general population. If there is good evidence that the condition: • was pre-existing and/or; • has been caused solely by exposure to agents outside work; and • was neither exacerbated nor triggered by exposure at work, the condition need not be reported.

Schedule 3, Part II

Regulation 5

Part II Diseases additionally reportable in respect of offshore workplaces

48 *Chickenpox.*

49 *Cholera.*

50 *Diptheria.*

51 *Dysentery (amoebic or bacillary).*

52 *Acute encephalitis.*

53 *Erysipelas.*

Schedule 3, Part II

54 *Food poisoning.*

55 *Legionellosis.*

56 *Malaria.*

57 *Measles.*

58 *Meningitis.*

59 *Meningococcal septicaemia (without meningitis).*

60 *Mumps.*

61 *Paratyphoid fever.*

62 *Plague.*

63 *Acute poliomyelitis.*

64 *Rabies.*

65 *Rubella.*

66 *Scarlet fever.*

67 *Tetanus.*

68 *Tuberculosis.*

69 *Typhoid fever.*

70 *Typhus.*

71 *Viral haemorrhagic fevers.*

72 *Viral hepatitis.*

Schedule 4 Records

Regulation 7

Schedule 4, Part I

Part I Particulars to be kept in records of any event which is reportable under regulation 3

1 *Date and time of the accident or dangerous occurrence.*

2 *In the event of an accident suffered by a person at work, the following particulars of that person -*

(a) *full name;*

(b) *occupation;*

(c) *nature of injury.*

3 *In the event of an accident suffered by a person not at work, the following particulars of that person (unless they are not known and it is not reasonably practicable to ascertain them) -*

(a) *full name;*

(b) *status (for example "passenger", "customer", "visitor" or "bystander");*

(c) *nature of injury.*

4 *Place where the accident or dangerous occurrence happened.*

5 *A brief description of the circumstances in which the accident or dangerous occurrence happened.*

6 *The date on which the event was first reported to the relevant enforcing authority.*

7 *The method by which the event was reported.*

Schedule 4, Part II

Part II Particulars to be kept in records of instances of any of the diseases specified in Schedule 3 and reportable under regulation 5

1 *Date of diagnosis of the disease.*

2 *Name of the person affected.*

3 *Occupation of the person affected.*

4 *Name or nature of the disease.*

5 *The date on which the disease was first reported to the relevant enforcing authority.*

6 *The method by which the disease was reported.*

Schedule 5

Additional provisions relating to mines and quarries

Regulation 8

Schedule

1 In this Schedule, unless the context otherwise requires -

"appropriate person" means -

(a) in the case of a coal mine, the responsible person or a person appointed in the management structure of that mine established pursuant to paragraph (1) of regulation 10 of the Management and Administration of Safety and Health at Mines Regulations 1993;

(b) in the case of any other mine, the responsible person;

(c) in the case of a quarry -

(i) the responsible person, or

(ii) (where there is a sole manager) that manager, or

(iii) (where there are two or more managers) the manager of the part of the quarry where the accident or dangerous occurrence happened, or

(iv) any person who is for the time being treated for the purposes of the Mines and Quarries Act 1954 as such a manager;

"nominated person" means the person (if any) who is for the time being nominated -

(a) in a case where there is an association or body representative of a majority of the total number of persons employed at a mine or quarry, by that association or body;

(b) in any other case, jointly by associations or bodies which are together representative of such a majority,

to receive on behalf of the persons so employed notices under this Schedule.

2 Where at a mine or a quarry any person, as a result of an accident arising out of or in connection with work, dies or suffers any major injury, or where there is a dangerous occurrence, the responsible person shall -

(a) forthwith notify the nominated person thereof by the quickest practicable means; and

(b) within 7 days send a report thereof to the nominated person on a form approved for the purposes of regulation 3.

3 Where there is a non-fatal injury to any person at a mine or quarry which is reported in accordance with paragraph 2, after which that person dies and his death is as a result of the accident then as soon as it comes to his knowledge the responsible person shall give notice of the death to the nominated person.

4 (1) Where there is an accident or dangerous occurrence in relation to which paragraph 2 applies no person shall disturb the place where it happened or tamper with anything at that place before -

5

(a) the expiration of 3 clear days after the matter to which paragraph 2 applies has been notified in accordance with these Regulations; or

(b) the place has been visited by an inspector and by workmen's inspectors exercising the powers conferred on them by section 123 of the Mines and Quarries Act 1954;

whichever is the sooner.

(2) Nothing in sub-paragraph (1) of this paragraph shall prohibit the doing of anything by or with the consent of an inspector.

(3) The requirements of sub-paragraph (1) of this paragraph shall not apply to an accident or to a dangerous occurrence if an appropriate person -

(a) has taken adequate steps to ascertain that disturbing the site -

(i) is unlikely to prejudice any investigation by an inspector into the circumstances of the accident or dangerous occurrence, and

(ii) is necessary to secure the safety of any person at the mine or quarry or to avoid disrupting the normal working thereof; and

(b) (except in the case of a non-fatal accident or a dangerous occurrence, where the nominated person or any person designated by that nominated person pursuant to this sub-paragraph cannot be contacted within a reasonable time) has notified the nominated person, or any person designated in writing by the nominated person to receive any such notification, of the proposed disturbance, and gives such a person a reasonable opportunity to visit the site before it is disturbed; and

(c) has taken adequate steps to ensure that there is obtained such information as will enable a full and accurate plan to be prepared forthwith, which plan shall show the position of any equipment or other item relevant to the accident or dangerous occurrence immediately after it happened; and

(d) ensures that any equipment or other item relevant to the accident or dangerous occurrence is kept as it was immediately after the incident until an inspector agrees that it may be disposed of.

(4) The person who has taken the steps referred to in sub-paragraph (3)(c) of this paragraph shall ensure that the plan referred to in that sub-paragraph is signed by the person who prepared it and bears the date on which it was prepared, and that a copy of that plan is supplied on request to any inspector or to the nominated person.

(5) It shall be a defence in proceedings against any person for contravening sub-paragraph (1) of this paragraph in any case which consists of the doing of any act, for that person to prove that the doing of that act was necessary for securing the safety of the mine or quarry or of any person.

5 The record kept under regulation 7, excluding any health record of an identifiable individual, shall be available for inspection by -

(a) the nominated person; and

5 *(b) workmen's inspectors exercising the powers conferred on them by section 123 of the Mines and Quarries Act 1954.*

Schedule 6

Additional provisions relating to offshore workplaces

Regulation 9

Schedule 6

Disturbance of site

1 (1) In any case where any person, as a result of an accident arising out of or in connection with work at an offshore workplace, dies or suffers a major injury, no person shall disturb the place where it happened or tamper with anything at that place before -

(a) the expiration of 3 clear days after the matter has been notified in accordance with these Regulations; or

(b) the place has been visited by an inspector;

whichever is the sooner.

(2) Nothing in sub-paragraph (1) of this paragraph shall prohibit the doing of anything by or with the consent of an inspector or the doing of anything necessary to secure the safety of the workplace or of any person, plant or vessel.

Enactments or instruments requiring the notification of events which are not required to be notified or reported under these Regulations

Regulation 10(4)

Schedule

7

1 *Title of Enactment or Instrument*	2 *Reference*
The Explosives Act 1875.	*1875 c.17.*
The Nuclear Installations Act 1965 and Orders and Regulations made or to be made thereunder.	*1965 c.57.*
The Merchant Shipping Act 1988 and Orders and Regulations made or to be made thereunder.	*1988 c.12.*
The Ionising Radiations Regulations 1985.	*S.I. 1985/1333.*
The Air Navigation (Investigation of Air Accidents involving Civil and Military Aircraft or Installations) Regulations 1986.	*S.I. 1986/1953.*
The Civil Aviation (Investigation of Air Accidents) Regulations 1989.	*S.I. 1989/2062.*

Schedule 8

Schedule

Regulation 15

Part I Revocations

Column 1 *Title of instrument*	*Column 2* *Reference*	*Column 3* *Extent of revocation*
The Reporting of Injuries, Diseases and Dangerous Occurrences Regulations 1985.	*S.I. 1985/2023.*	*The whole Regulations.*
The Reporting of Injuries, Diseases and Dangerous Occurrences (Amendment) Regulations 1989.	*S.I. 1989/1457.*	*The whole Regulations.*
The Offshore Installations (Inspectors and Casualties) Regulations 1973.	*S.I. 1973/1842.*	*Part II and the Schedule; and the entry relating to "disease" in regulation 1(2).*
The Submarine Pipe-lines (Inspectors etc.) Regulations 1977.	*S.I. 1977/835.*	*Regulations 5 and 6, the reference to regulations 5 and 6 in regulation 7(1)(a),and Schedule 2.*
The Railways (Notice of Accidents) Order 1986.	*S.I. 1986/2187.*	*The whole Order.*
The Offshore Installations (Amendment) Regulations 1991.	*S.I. 1991/679.*	*The whole Regulations.*

8, Part I

Schedule

Part II Amendments

1 In regulations 3(4)(c) and 7(5)(b) of the Mines (Safety of Exit) Regulations 1988 for the words "Schedule 4 to the Reporting of Injuries, Diseases and Dangerous Occurrences Regulations 1985 "there shall be substituted the words "Schedule 5 to the Reporting of Injuries, Diseases and Dangerous Occurrences Regulations 1995".

2 In regulation 17 (6) of the Offshore Installations (Safety Representatives and Safety Committees) Regulations 1989 for the words after "means" there shall be substituted the words "any death, injury, disease or dangerous occurrence which is required to be reported under the Reporting of Injuries, Diseases or Dangerous Occurrences Regulations 1995".

8, Part II

Appendix 1

HSE area offices

HSE area offices (Open 9 am to 5 pm Monday to Friday)

Contact addresses and telephone numbers

Inter City House, Mitchell Lane, Victoria Street, BRISTOL BS1 6AN
Tel: 0117 988 6000 (Fax: 0117 926 2998)
Covers - Avon, Cornwall, Devon, Gloucestershire, Somerset, Isles of Scilly

Priestley House, Priestley Road, BASINGSTOKE RG24 9NW
Tel: 01256 404000 (Fax: 01256 404 120)
Covers - Berkshire, Dorset, Hampshire, Isle of Wight, Wiltshire

3 East Grinstead House, London Road, EAST GRINSTEAD RH19 1RR
Tel: 01342 334 200 (Fax: 01342 334 222)
Covers - Kent, Surrey, East Sussex, West Sussex

Maritime House, 1 Linton Road, BARKING IG11 8HF
Tel: 0181 235 8000 (Fax: 0181 235 8001)
Covers - Barking and Dagenham, Barnet, Brent, Camden, Ealing, Enfield, Hackney, Haringey, Harrow, Havering, Islington, Newham, Redbridge, Tower Hamlets, Waltham Forest

1 Long Lane, LONDON SE1 4PG
Tel: 0171 556 2100 (Fax: 0171 556 2200)
Covers - Bexley, Bromley, City of London, Croydon, Greenwich, Hammersmith and Fulham, Hillingdon, Hounslow, Kensington and Chelsea, Kingston, Lambeth, Lewisham, Merton, Richmond, Southwark, Sutton, Wandsworth, Westminster

39 Baddow Road, CHELMSFORD CM2 0HL
Tel: 01245 706 200 (Fax: 01245 706 222)
Covers - Essex (except the London Boroughs in Essex covered by the Barking Office), Norfolk, Suffolk

14 Cardiff Road, LUTON LU1 1PP
Tel: 01582 444200 (Fax: 01582 444320)
Covers - Bedfordshire, Buckinghamshire, Cambridgeshire, Hertfordshire

Belgrave House, 1 Greyfriars, NORTHAMPTON NN1 2BS
Tel: 01604 738300 (Fax: 01604 738333)
Covers - Leicestershire, Northamptonshire, Oxfordshire, Warwickshire

McLaren Building, 35 Dale End, BIRMINGHAM B4 7NP
Tel: 0121 609 5200 (Fax: 0121 609 5349)
Covers - Birmingham, Coventry, Dudley, Sandwell, Solihull, Walsall, Wolverhampton

Brunel House, 2 Fitzalan Road, CARDIFF CF2 1SH
Tel: 01222 263 000(Fax: 01222 263 120)
Covers - Clwyd, Dyfed, Gwent, Gwynedd, Mid Glamorgan, Powys, South Glamorgan, West Glamorgan

The Marches House, Midway, NEWCASTLE-UNDER-LYME ST5 1DT
Tel: 01782 602 300 (Fax: 01782 602 400)
Covers - Hereford and Worcester, Shropshire, Staffordshire

The Pearsons Building 55 Upper Parliament Street NOTTINGHAM NG1 6AU
Tel: 0115 971 2800 (Fax: 0115 971 2802)
Covers - Derbyshire, Lincolnshire, Nottinghamshire

Sovereign House, 110 Queen Street, SHEFFIELD S1 2ES
Tel: 0114 273 9081 (Fax: 01142 912 379)
Covers - Barnsley, Doncaster, Humberside, Rotherham, Sheffield

8 St Paul's Street, LEEDS LS1 2LE
Tel: 0113 283 4200 (Fax: 0113 283 4296)
Covers - Bradford, Calderdale, Kirklees, Leeds, Wakefield, Craven, Hambleton, Harrogate, Richmondshire, Ryedale, Scarborough, Selby, York

Quay House, Quay Street, MANCHESTER M3 3JB
Tel: 0161 952 8200 (Fax: 0161 952 8222)
Covers - Bolton, Bury, City of Manchester, City of Salford, Oldham, Rochdale, Stockport, Tameside, Trafford, Wigan

The Triad, Stanley Road, BOOTLE, Merseyside L20 3PG
Tel: 0151 479 2200(Fax: 0151 479 2201)
Covers - Chester, Congleton, Crewe, Ellesmere Port, Halton, Knowsley, Liverpool, Macclesfield, St Helens, Sefton, Vale Royal, Warrington, Wirral

Victoria House, Ormskirk Road, PRESTON PR1 1HH
Tel: 01772 836 200(Fax: 01772 836 222)
Covers - Cumbria, Lancashire

Arden House, Regent Centre, Regent Farm Road, Gosforth, NEWCASTLE-UPON-TYNE NE3 3JN
Tel: 0191 202 6200 (Fax: 0191 202 6300)
Covers - Cleveland, Durham, Newcastle-upon-Tyne, Northumberland, North Tyneside, South Tyneside, Sunderland

Belford House, 59 Belford Road, EDINBURGH EH4 3UE
Tel: 0131 247 2000 (Fax: 0131 247 2121)
Covers - Borders, Central, Fife, Grampian, Highland, Lothian, Tayside, Orkney and Shetland

375 West George Street, GLASGOW G2 4LW
Tel: 0141 275 3000 (Fax: 0141 275 3100)
Covers - Dumfries and Galloway, Strathclyde, and the Western Isles

HSE Offshore Safety Division Offices

Lord Cullen House, Fraser Place, Aberdeen AB1 1UB
Tel: 01224 252500
Fax: 01224 252577

122A Thorpe Road, Norwich NR1 1RN
Tel: 01603 275000
Fax: 01603 275050

Merton House, Stanley Road, Bootle, Liverpool L20 3DL
Tel: 0151 951 4000
Fax: 0151 951 3158

HM Inspectorate of Mines district offices

Scotland & East England District Office
Silver House, Silver Street,Doncaster Yorkshire DN1 9HR
Tel: 10302 368165/342267
Fax: 01302 326 521

Wales and West England District Office
St Annes House, University Road, Bootle, L20 3RA
Tel: 0151 951 3991
Fax; 0151 951 3896

HSE Information Centres

Sheffield Information Centre
(Open 9 am to 5 pm, Monday to Friday, to phone and personal callers)
Health and Safety Executive, Information Centre, Broad Lane,
SHEFFIELD S3 7HQ
Tel: 0114 289 2345 (Fax: 0114 289 2333)

London Information Centre
(Open 9 am to 5 pm, Monday to Friday, to personal callers only) Health and Safety Executive, Information Centre, Rose Court, 2 Southwark Bridge, LONDON SE1 9HS

Bootle Information Centre
(Open 9 am to 5 pm, Monday to Friday, to personal callers only) Health and Safety Executive, Information Centre, St Hugh's House, Stanley Precinct, BOOTLE, Merseyside L20 3QY

Health and Safety at Work etc Act 1974
The Reporting of Injuries, Diseases and Dangerous Occurrences Regulations 1995

HSE Health & Safety Executive

Report of an injury or dangerous occurrence

Filling in this form
This form must be filled in by an employer or other responsible person.

Part A

About you

1 What is your full name?

2 What is your job title?

3 What is your telephone number?

About your organisation

4 What is the name of your organisation?

5 What is its address and postcode?

6 What type of work does the organisation do?

Part B

About the incident

1 On what date did the incident happen?

/ /

2 At what time did the incident happen?
(Please use the 24-hour clock eg 0600)

3 Did the incident happen at the above address?

Yes ☐ Go to question 4

No ☐ Where did the incident happen?

☐ elsewhere in your organisation – give the name, address and postcode

☐ at someone else's premises – give the name, address and postcode

☐ in a public place – give details of where it happened

If you do not know the postcode, what is the name of the local authority?

4 In which department, or where on the premises, did the incident happen?

Part C

About the injured person

If you are reporting a dangerous occurrence, go to Part F.
If more than one person was injured in the same incident, please attach the details asked for in Part C and Part D for each injured person.

1 What is their full name?

2 What is their home address and postcode?

3 What is their home phone number?

4 How old are they?

5 Are they

☐ male?

☐ female?

6 What is their job title?

7 Was the injured person (tick only one box)

☐ one of your employees?

☐ on a training scheme? Give details:

☐ on work experience?

☐ employed by someone else? Give details of the employer:

☐ self-employed and at work?

☐ a member of the public?

Part D

About the injury

1 What was the injury? (eg fracture, laceration)

2 What part of the body was injured?

F2508 (01/96)

Continued overleaf

3 Was the injury (tick the one box that applies)

- ☐ a fatality?
- ☐ a major injury or condition? (see accompanying notes)
- ☐ an injury to an employee or self-employed person which prevented them doing their normal work for more than 3 days?
- ☐ an injury to a member of the public which meant they had to be taken from the scene of the accident to a hospital for treatment?

4 Did the injured person (tick all the boxes that apply)

- ☐ become unconscious?
- ☐ need resuscitation?
- ☐ remain in hospital for more than 24 hours?
- ☐ none of the above.

Part E

About the kind of accident

Please tick the one box that best describes what happened, then go to Part G.

- ☐ Contact with moving machinery or material being machined
- ☐ Hit by a moving, flying or falling object
- ☐ Hit by a moving vehicle
- ☐ Hit something fixed or stationary

- ☐ Injured while handling, lifting or carrying
- ☐ Slipped, tripped or fell on the same level
- ☐ Fell from a height

  How high was the fall?

  ________ metres

- ☐ Trapped by something collapsing

- ☐ Drowned or asphyxiated
- ☐ Exposed to, or in contact with, a harmful substance
- ☐ Exposed to fire
- ☐ Exposed to an explosion

- ☐ Contact with electricity or an electrical discharge
- ☐ Injured by an animal
- ☐ Physically assaulted by a person

- ☐ Another kind of accident (describe it in Part G)

Part F

Dangerous occurrences

Enter the number of the dangerous occurrence you are reporting. (The numbers are given in the Regulations and in the notes which accompany this form.)

☐

Part G

Describing what happened

Give as much detail as you can. For instance

- the name of any substance involved
- the name and type of any machine involved
- the events that led to the incident
- the part played by any people.

If it was a personal injury, give details of what the person was doing. Describe any action that has since been taken to prevent a similar incident. Use a separate piece of paper if you need to.

☐

Part H

Your signature

Signature

☐

Date

/ /

Where to send the form

Please send it to the Enforcing Authority for the place where it happened. If you do not know the Enforcing Authority, send it to the nearest HSE office.

For official use			
Client number	Location number	Event number	☐ INV REP ☐ Y ☐ N

Health and Safety at Work etc Act 1974
The Reporting of Injuries, Diseases and Dangerous Occurrences Regulations 1995

HSE Health & Safety Executive

Report of a case of disease

Filling in this form

This form must be filled in by an employer or other responsible person.

Part A

About you

1 What is your full name?

2 What is your job title?

3 What is your telephone number?

About your organisation

4 What is the name of your organisation?

5 What is its address and postcode?

6 Does the affected person usually work at this address?

Yes ☐ Go to question 7

No ☐ Where do they normally work?

7 What type of work does the organisation do?

Part B

About the affected person

1 What is their full name?

2 What is their date of birth?

/ /

3 What is their job title?

4 Are they

☐ male?

☐ female?

5 Is the affected person (tick one box)

☐ one of your employees?

☐ on a training scheme? Give details:

☐ on work experience?

☐ employed by someone else? Give details:

☐ other? Give details:

F2508A (01/96)

Continued overleaf

Part C

The disease you are reporting

1 Please give:

- the name of the disease, and the type of work it is associated with; or
- the name and number of the disease (from Schedule 3 of the Regulations – see the accompanying notes).

2 What is the date of the statement of the doctor who first diagnosed or confirmed the disease?

/ /

3 What is the name and address of the doctor?

Part D

Describing the work that led to the disease

Please describe any work done by the affected person which might have led to them getting the disease.

If the disease is thought to have been caused by exposure to an agent at work (eg a specific chemical) please say what that agent is.

Give any other information which is relevant.

Give your description here

Continue your description here

Part E

Your signature

Signature

Date

/ /

Where to send the form

Please send it to the Enforcing Authority for the place where the affected person works. If you do not know the Enforcing Authority, send it to the nearest HSE office.

For official use

Client number

Location number

Event number

☐ INV REP ☐ Y ☐ N

Appendix 3

References

1 *Everyone's guide to RIDDOR '95* HSE 31 1996 HSE Books, available in packs of 10 ISBN 0 7176 1077 2

2 *A guide for railways, tramways, trolley vehicle systems and other guided transport systems on the Reporting of Injuries, Diseases and Dangerous Occurrences Regulations 1995* 1996 HSE Books ISBN 0 7176 1022 5

3 *The Management of Health and Safety at Work* Approved Code of Practice L21 1992 HMSO ISBN 0 7176 0412 8

4 *Combined pad of F2508 and F2508A* 1996 HSE Books ISBN 0 7176 1078 0

5 *Electronic versions of F2508 and F2508A combined with A Guide to the Reporting of injuries, diseases and dangerous occurrences Regulations 1995* 1996 HSE Books ISBN 0 7176 1080 2

6 *Safety representative and safety committees* 1988 HSE Books ISBN 0 11 883959 4

7 *Categorisation of biological agents according to hazard and categories of containment* 1995 HSE Books ISBN 0 7176 1038 1

8 *Hand-arm vibration* HS(G)88 1994 HSE Books ISBN 0 7176 0743 7

9 *Health surveillance of occupational skin disease* MS24 1991 ISBN 0 11 885583 2

10 *Preventing asthma at work* L55 1994 HSE Books ISBN 0 7176 0661 9

Printed and published by the Health and Safety Executive C200 1/96